McGauran's Beach

Written by

S. Lewis-Campbell
(Based on a true story)

<u>Disclaimer</u>

Some personal details have been changed for privacy.

Preface

If you have found yourself on this page, I would like to welcome you to my first official novel. Although I have been avidly writing for the past four years, I would consider myself a relatively new writer still adjusting to the confinements and opinions of those, whose role is to scrutinize and harshly critique my work. Most would find this approach to be in complete contrast to that of a budding Author, as I continue to grow in this area I hope I am able to overcome this aspect or at least develop a thicker skin in the future. I took the decision to write this novel for many reasons; four months before completing the manuscript "Grimm's Law"; I felt a strong impulse to write a Romance, a genre I initially felt I would have very little interest in. I could not understand the strong compulsion to write from such a prospective or the reason for it at the time, however whatever the cause it was significantly apparent that I had very few positive examples, I felt inspired by to draw upon.

The majority of my work is derived from personal experience and is the main principal adopted for my interpretation of producing creative narrative. Being able to relate, or to feel personally affected by an event and to be able to document it on paper, provides the basis to be able to write an honest account from a palpable view point. Creatively this aspect was considered essential in being able to execute this piece; being able to offer a personable account assisted in being able to maintain the interests and perceptions of the reader. Being my first novel I wanted to create a body of work that was as authentic as possible and made an early decision to depict the main character in third-person as a matter of discourse. At times maintaining this literary style was considerably ambitious, however I have learnt throughout this experience is if I did not live to experience it then I would be unable to tell it.

Finally, I would like to thank you the reader for selecting this novel and whatever your reasons were for doing so, I am very grateful.

S. Lewis-Campbell.

Australia

She never would have guessed that such good fortune would be bestowed upon her; there she was just simply minding her own business, attempting to be as insignificant as possible albeit in an unacquainted setting; being the only individual present from her descent coupled with her unashamedly distinctive appearance, the more she attempted to blend in to the background, the more she appeared to stick out like a sore thumb. In less than a week, following her initial contact with Hita, her plane tickets to Melbourne, Australia had been booked and her visa sorted, there would be no going back on her decision now, never mind the disappointment she would cause Hita and her family who were eagerly anticipating her arrival. Hita had initially invited her over to visit with a view to moving out there on a more permanent basis almost ten years ago;   keen to ensure a positive future for both her best friend and daughter Tia. Hita had been indoctrinated as an 'unofficial Godmother' to Tia more than twenty years ago, however without the pomp and ceremony.

Hita and her then boyfriend Simon would routinely pop round to her place with normally stay overnight; the four of them had formed their own unit, having first met as students after enrolling at Southbank University. The foursome had developed a close and special bond, and spent a lot of their time together, both in London and in Leicester where Hita's family lived. Twenty-one years later life had changed drastically for them over the years and in many aspects the changes had been for the better.

As a mother she felt she had done the best job possible and Tia was a credit to her, however her personal life was a complete shambles. Her existing relationship had been on the decline for at least four years, she should have been celebrating seven blissful years together, instead the cold reality was she had been unhappy with the relationship almost two years in to it. She had chosen to put her personal feelings to one side, owing to the guilt she felt for upsetting the family unit she had created. She had confided to Hita about how she felt at the time, yet Hita liked Grimm and thought they were good together and hoped they would be able to resolve any issues. Ending the relationship at that time would have resulted in dissolving Grimm's first ever relationship, as well as her daughter's first experience of having two Guardians living under the same roof. Although the situation was not ideal, she did not want to over complicate matters, realising the two individuals that stood to be most affected appeared close and quite content with the current arrangements.

She often noticed them laughing and enjoying time together, even if it meant at the expense of her own happiness. They enjoyed catching up at the end of the working day and vivaciously making fun of the woman who was central to them both. She did not have it within her to interfere in their relationship, nor did she want to be the cause of disrupting a bond between two individuals, who held a genuine fondness for one another. She thought it would be best to let the situation remain as it was and hoped she would be able to go along with it until Tia left home; she felt that would be the perfect time to end her relationship with Grimm with the minimal amount of disruption.

The breakdown of the relationship had been determined by various factors, in particular Grimm's lack of discretion. He had a common habit of regurgitating all aspects of their relationship, to anyone that was interested in listening. As Grimm thought it, he said it and by doing so it caused her an extreme amount of embarrassment, especially if she ever came in to contact with any of his associates. One friend in particular, Dan had a front row seat and knew about her every move, including any issues they had at home. Dan even had an inside view regarding her future plans, even more so than she did. Whenever another embarrassing revelation occurred, she would contact Grimm immediately to complain, normally resulting in to a huge argument whereby Grimm would constantly deny the accusations. Grimm had no control over his tongue and it developed in to a major issue for her, although she pleaded with him, Grimm was unable to help himself which caused a major rift within their relationship.

An even bigger issue were some of Grimm's friends, some would often attempt to kiss her inappropriately whenever she visited or would make perverse comments to her in Grimm's absence. She would often complain to Grimm about that type of behaviour being unacceptable to her and she felt uncomfortable around them. Grimm refused to speak to his friends about their behaviour and instead told her to ignore it and passed it off as being harmless. Grimm's friend Dan had no boundaries and would often vilify his own partner Yvonne in the presence of others. Yvonne was the constant butt of his salacious jokes usually centred on her weight or unsavoury comments about her appearance; he had no decorum and often degraded the mother of his two children on a regular basis. Dan thought his comedy was hilarious, even at the expense of their young daughters, yet Yvonne would never do anything to prevent it. She felt ashamed for Yvonne and grew tired of the constant battles with Grimm, due to his lack of discernment. Grimm's lack of consideration regarding her feelings was responsible for damaging their relationship the most. Grimm would usually just shrug his shoulders, looking completely helpless and at a loss for words. His inability to manage the situation like a real man ought to have done only further damaged their relationship.

Things became irreparable a few months later when Dan would go on to steal money from her Mother, following a poor car service. At the time Dan had confided to Grimm about not refunding the money her Mother had been due and asked Grim for his opinion on the matter. Grim chose to support Dan rather than encourage him to do the right thing by paying her Mother what she was owed. It was at that time Grimm had told her of the situation when she made the decision, that the relationship was completely over and that this level of utter disrespect would no longer be tolerated. From that moment on she made the transition of protecting her own personal interests, until their day of reckoning came.

In addition to their already dwindling relationship were the impending redundancies at Grimm's work. The company was closing down its London office where Grimm had been based over fifteen years, following a company merger. The company was relocating to Peterborough and Grimm's position would be instrumental during the transitional period. Grimm would mainly be working out of the Peterborough site, until the restructure were in place the transition was expected to take eighteen months to complete.

The day before Grimm's forty-fourth birthday he arrived in London to begin his birthday celebrations, although things within the relationship were still very fragmented, birthdays were considered important occasions to be celebrated. Grimm had travelled back to

London with his Mother Liz in tow from Peterborough. He had not been expected to return to London and always informed them beforehand when Liz would be visiting. This would ensure they had plenty of food brought in and the house would be ready to receive guests.

Grimm spent the majority of his time in Peterborough and only visited London on occasional weekends. She had been out with Tia at the time finalising some of the treats they had arranged for Grimm's birthday. Shortly after returning home, they noticed the birthday cards Grimm had received at work. Grimm had displayed three of the birthday cards in the living room, and had opened a selection of gifts he had been given leaving the empty gift bags and wrapping papers in an untidy heap discarded on the Living Room floor beside him. She picked up the birthday card positioned closest to her and opened it, the card had a photo of a monkey on the outside and included the usual cheeky birthday messages from some of his work colleagues. As she began reading the second card, the amused expression of her face began to change from one of amusement to one of complete disgust as she read the message contained inside. The message stated 'Happy Birthday to my Work Husband' and continued to the effect of, 'Yes, you will always be my work husband and I couldn't care less what my actual husband has to say about it' and signed 'I love you'.

To say she was shocked by what she had read was a complete understatement, how she managed to compose herself after reading the second birthday card, even she had trouble comprehending. Liz and Tia, who were also seated in the living room with Grimm at the time, were also beginning to wonder what was written in the card. The third card was from Suzanne who was considered a colleague and friend to them both. Suzanne's card offered an outpouring of how much she also loved Grimm and noted whilst she was unable to compete with the standard of amorous poems he sent her daily. Suzanne had attempted to recite one of her own, which resulted in a detailed declaration of her personal feelings towards him. She quickly realised Grimm had not been excusing the scheduled weekend visits to London they had previously arranged, was not due to his work commitments. The real reason Grimm had been too busy to visit her at the weekends, for the majority of the eighteen months he had been based in Peterborough, was due to professing his undivided love and affection towards the female colleagues at his job. According to the messages contained in the cards, the female colleagues all appeared to welcome the flirtatious attention Grimm had been subjecting them to.

Her initial reaction was to ask him direct, yet she was still in shock as to whether this was a genuine situation or a prank. Grimm's character could be quite devious at times; however he didn't have it within him to be a philanderer of such proportions. Grimm confirmed it was no prank, both Tia and Liz were now concerned, although they also seemed too shocked to speak as they watch the events unfold, they could tell by her expression how dire the situation was quickly becoming. Her responses confirmed this matter was no longer considered a laughing matter as it may have appeared to them initially. Grimm had no misgivings in showcasing the cards around the living room without even a thought for her. She turned to Liz and enquired whether she had been aware of Grimm's declarations of love and questioned whether she had read the cards. Liz's response having witnessed the events play out before her was of utter shock and disbelief. She advised Grimm that any previous plans she had made regarding his birthday had since been cancelled and duly walked out of the living room with Tia in tow. Tia was just as appalled as she had been, although she didn't have all the facts; she was aware her mum had been undeservedly disrespected.

Armed with all the evidence she needed, she no longer began making an effort to spend time with Grimm whenever he returned to the home. In fact, she made a point of them never being in the same room together, unless she deemed it absolutely necessary. They had been sleeping in separate beds for years, over time this set up had become a permanent arrangement. Grimm had been relinquished to the sitting room whenever he returned home, not that he seemed to mind. She began socialising regularly with work colleagues, by doing so she felt it aided her to forget the humiliation she had suffered. For her it was nothing more than a moment of escapism from the crappy relationship she now found herself a part of. She enjoyed drinking but it did not seem to like her as much, she was considered a lightweight with alcohol and after only a couple of cocktails, she would emerge in to being the happiest soul at the bar. Anyone outside the family home had no inkling of the issues between them; the one person she could genuinely confide in was Hita, but she didn't think it was fair to burden her with her problems.

She had come to a decision following the birth of Hita's first born Nile; that she would no longer take up Hita's time with her problems. This change was essential because she wanted their time to be about meaningful new memories, as the dynamics of their relationship took on yet another change for the better. Most of all she wanted Hita to have the chance to bond with Nile, just as she had done with Tia when she was first born. During the ten years Hita had resided in Australia their friendship had continued to evolve over the years as they matured. Their friendship had started whilst they were both attended the same University and studied the same Degree. Thereafter Hita had gone on to complete her

Masters and Doctorate, eventually securing a transfer to Melbourne, Australia as part of a secondment with her job, the move only made their friendship stronger and Hita would visit often during her yearly return trips to the UK. Hita's family resided in Leicester, whenever she visited with Paul who she'd met in Australia they would stay with her when in London, by doing so it allowed Hita and Tia time to catch up. She couldn't have been happier for Hita when she completed her PhD and soon began working in her desired role as a Criminal Psychologist; she had been around at the time when the reality had just been a dream of Hita's. She was so proud of her attainments, having witnessed her work so diligently, yet singlehandedly to achieve such accolades and Hita had achieved it all without even stopping for breath in between.

***

The transition at Grimm's work had been going ahead successfully; however his relationship was at a new all-time low, following the exposure of his illicit flirting. Grimm decided to up the ante by moving in to a female colleague's home. He had taken the decision to move in to Mena's without bothering to consult the members of his existing household back in London. He had only involved her regarding the redundancy package, whereby staff from the London site had been given the option of purchasing a property in Peterborough as part of their settlement, later this offer was retracted company retracted by the company who instead were now only prepared to offer two property rentals for the London staff to share until the restructure transition was completed. Grimm was not happy with the decisions being made by the company and in turn decided to take up residency with Mena, without bothering to inform his girlfriend back in London. In fact, the only time Grimm bothered to seek the consent of his partner was leading up to the transition. Although his move to

Peterborough would be inconvenient to her, she did not have the heart to prevent Grimm from fulfilling his wishes.

In addition to running the house on her own with Grimm gone, she had the added task of completing the recent renovation work she had undertaken at home. She also held down a full time job as a Senior Personal Assistant and had a daughter who still lived with her to consider. Grimm had promised if she allowed him to complete the restructure, he would reward for her with a well-earned all expenses paid holiday to a destination of her choice. Tia was also expected to accompany them, providing she could take the time off work. The main point of the holiday would be to discuss the issues between them, away from the pressures of their normal environment. With the transition completed early December 2015, Grimm returned to London. Things remained extremely strained between them; her mind was firmly fixed on the humiliation from the previous months, meanwhile Grimm was focused on not having a job and catching up on his rest, yet he had not been prepared for the awkward response he received from the family following his return.

The relationship was completely over in her mind, now that Grimm had returned to London she began organising the trip she had been promised and decided on a trip to Jamaica. She hadn't been for a few years and recalled Grimm had previously expressed a keen interest in visiting the island. She thought it would be the ideal place for them to visit and inform him of her decision for them to separate. She found an all-inclusive holiday and was about to confirm the booking when Tia confirmed her intentions of joining them on the trip. Halfway during a new holiday search for three instead of two, Tia later retracted her decision to go join them after realising she would not be able to get the time off work in time for January 2016, when they had planned to travel. In the time it took for Tia's change of heart and her attempts to retrieve the former all-inclusive break she had previously seen, the offer no longer appeared to exist. Desperate to track down the original online offer she contacted Hays and Jarvis direct who recalled the offer, except the price had now escalated to an astronomical £8999.00. She decided at that point to abandon the search for the day and revisit at it again when she was less perturbed.

A week or two later, it had become evident that Grimm was struggling to adjust to being back in London post Peterborough. Not only had he returned to sleeping on the sofa-bed in the living room and the house being empty during the day. He found he had lots of free time available which he spent doing nothing. A couple of weeks later his temperament changed in to one of boredom and being short tempered. On hindsight it was probably a cry for attention at the time; unable to read his mind she chose to ignore him for the time being. Grimm had also stopped taking care of himself; his clothes were often found strewn around the living room for up to weeks at a time. It was evident he was having trouble coping with his new found freedom; she approached him about it having discerned the declined state of the living room. It was particularly becoming an issue when guests came to visit, or the lack of visitors due to the state of the place. She wanted to know about his future plans, as the current living arrangements were not ideal; she was not used to her place looking in such a state and was having trouble accepting her home looking the way that it was.

Grimm declared he had no plans to look for work, and planned to take a two month break, before seeking employment. She didn't agree with his plans and thought his ideas were for the most part irresponsible and out of the question. Over the years Grimm had become so far removed from the person she had first met, she barely recognised him. He had struck her as quite generous when they had first met and could not do enough for her to show how much she meant to him, seven years later he had become overly frugal and the emphasis was more about money, rather than their relationship. It suddenly dawned on her Grimm had not brought her flowers, or anything for that matter outside of her birthday and the last time he had was at least four years ago. She realised she no longer recognised or even liked this person he had turned in to. She attempted to reason with him, and suggested the two month break he was planning on taking off, did not pose as a problem within itself, but to not look for work during those two months was a foolish idea and certainly not an example she wanted Tia to follow and suggested he begin searching for a new job sooner, rather than later and when successful with a position he could always negotiate a delayed start date if he so wished. Grimm ignored her advice and continued on embarking on his two month hiatus, seven months after Grimm was still without work and now desperate to find employment. Although she was supportive during his search she felt the fault was his own for simply choosing to ignore her invaluable advice at the time, more evidently he was certainly living up to his new nickname she had given him 'Ignoramus.'

She had always been upfront with Grimm about preferring to discuss their issues in private; she felt it was unfair to upset the family dynamics. She was keen for Tia to be as unaffected as possible by their problems and it was important to her that Tia did not become embroiled in the personal problems. However, Grimm was having great difficulty keeping to it his end. She had just arrived home from work one evening when Grimm approached her out of the blue and informed her of his intentions to officially end the relationship and move out. Her response began with a curt "That's fine Grimm, like we had previously agreed we can discuss it on holiday, rather than now with Tia present." She was reluctant to continue with the untimely conversation, as it would involve a deeper discussion and arrangements put in place ahead of Grimm's departure. For her it was not as simple as just ending the relationship, there were lots of things that would needed to be finalised thereafter and she didn't feel the timing, was appropriate having just walked in from a hard day's work, she was exhausted and really needed a rest before she could begin dealing with stuff at home. Grimm had other plans and wanted to pursue the conversation right there and then oblivious to how she may have been feeling.

She felt strongly about not being in the right head space to cope with Grimm's outburst, not only was she being consistently bullied and harassed at work, she was also covering for two other colleagues who were both on long-term sick leave in her department and she was struggling to cope with the extra responsibilities. This was all becoming too much for her; she explained this to Grimm who showed no signs of understanding. With the realisation Grimm would continue on in this vain regardless of how she was feeling at the time. She desperately needed a break and made the decision to visit Hita in Australia. Hita had been in contact just a few days earlier, following the birth of her second son Ashton only ten days before. She felt she would be better served going to Australia for some much needed down-time, but only if Hita was completely sure she would be up to having her. Immediately after confirming her travel arrangements, Hita enquired why she had chosen to travel alone; she had expected Grimm to accompany her. She attempted to explain it away, and stated she felt it was for the best with Ashton only just being born. Hita was not buying in to it; she remembered their previous discussions about her no longer being happy. At the time

Hita had hoped it was just a blip and that they were working on resolving things between them.

She hated giving Hita bad news and that had often been the case the past few years, she also felt guilty for it and often found herself evading Hita at times, just to avoid her questions altogether. She updated Grimm regarding the new travel arrangements and although he seemed genuinely disappointed with the change of plans, he understood he was particularly at fault and accepted the new arrangements. With the decision made and the ticket booked she began to feel relieved and quite excited about the impending journey. Travelling to what seemed like the furthest part of the world; she considered it would be the ultimate travel experience. Travelling was by far her favourite hobby; she enjoyed the whole experience of travelling to another country, especially countries she had never visited before. She reflected how life had changed so drastically for her. Life had become unbearably limited since meeting Grimm; no longer did they travel together every year, often first class. In fact, over the past seven years she had not been on any holidays with Tia. Any vacations had either been with Grimm or with Grimm and his family.

She had mentioned to Grimm about her yearly holidays when they had first got together, Grimm dampened her spirits when he informed her she would not be able to afford that lifestyle anymore. Thereafter anytime she mentioned anything that involved an activity outside of their own four walls; Grimm did his best to dissuade her enthusiasm with the usual declaration, "Don't expect me to pay for it". She surmised Grimm as nothing more than a dream killer; his idea of a good time was turning a blind eye to the sexual prowess of his peers. She began to view him less than the man he had once claimed to be and more than likely the reason she had been his first partner at the grand old age of thirty-seven.

How had she managed to get involved with such a hot mess? She was determined not to allow the situation between them to continue as it was, things would need to change and with immediate effect.

***

Grimm had begun to notice a positive change in her attitude, to him she even began to resemble the confident woman he had first seen the first time they had met. She would be boarding the plane at five in the evening and would land in Melbourne during the early hours of the morning two days later. Grimm had insisted on accompanying her to the airport, little did they know it would be one of their final exchanges as a result of her trip. She felt re-energised and quite excited for her impending new adventure. She had packed for the trip weeks ago, however her female intuition had her dashing around the shops in a last minute dash in search of the few remaining items she thought she might need. She had no idea what to expect when she got there and thought it was best to have every eventuality covered just in case. She couldn't believe she was on her way to Australia and she suspected Hita had to be feeling the same. In the ten years it had been since Hita had moved there, this had been the third occasion Hita had so graciously asked her to visit. The first time she had asked her was a year after the move, at the time it had taken Hita a while to adjust to the new surroundings and it had taken her a full nine months to make a definite decision that she would move there herself permanently. The second time Hita had invited her to visit, Tia had just started secondary school and therefore the timing had not been suitable. Hita knew more than anyone what she had been through in trying to raise Tia on her own, she had sacrificed so much of herself just to raise her with very little assistance, Hita thought she deserved the opportunity to better herself and with her comfortably settled she was keen for her best friend to join her. The very thought of Hita considering her in that way, resonated strongly with her at a time when she felt no one else seemed to care.

As she boarded the plane for the first leg of the journey, she felt a combination of excitement and surrealism. In typical fashion Grimm had almost caused her to miss her flight, she could not bear to think how that would have materialised had she missed it. Grimm had insisted on them going for a meal straight after she had checked-in. The flight had been held for her as she did her best Usain Bolt impression and ran as fast as she could to make the flight once through customs, resulting in her being the last passenger to arrive on board. Upon entering the aircraft she was instantly escorted to a window seat and she slumped in to it as quickly as possible, to avoid the prying eyes of the few she believed to be disgruntled passengers seated nearby. By the time she had fastened her seat belt, the Muslim prayer being played on-board was well underway and the aircraft had already begun the early manoeuvres of positioning itself along the concourse in preparation of the long-haul flight whilst the aircraft attendants prepared for take-off. Feeling relatively familiar with her surroundings since her last flight three years prior, she began to take in the views during her favourite part of the journey, the ascent. Once the plane was enshrouded by clouds it would be the ideal time to dim the lights and switch on the inflight entertainment, most of which she ended up replaying repeatedly; as the programmes resulted in watching her as she nodded off during the course of them. Whenever she travelled she often used the flight as a way of catching up on some well-deserved uninterrupted sleep.

After some considerable time during the flight she felt her arm being shaken gently, she quickly gathered herself together and noticed the airline attendant attempting to get her attention. The attendant was a very striking in her appearance and modestly dressed; she informed her had become concerned about her welfare after boarding and offered her a range of beverages and delicacies that had been offered to the other passengers earlier. Although she hadn't understood all the options being suggested, she agreed to all the choices presented, still very much in a state of semi-consciousness and an even greater desire to continue sleeping. She struggled to eat the on-board cuisine and thought about Tia and Grimm she had left behind, she had told no one other than her immediate household and Dad she would be away. Despite all she had gone through recently she hadn't envisaged she would be the one to leave home so suddenly, considering Grimm had been the first to begin creating a new life for himself outside of the family home.

Soon after eating the halal meal she had been served, she realised she had no idea of what it was she had just eaten and quickly decided against obtaining a recipe to indulge in the future. She flicked through the in-flight entertainment packages and opted for one of the latest movie releases the offered, 'The Intern' starring Robert De Niro. She would go on to play it repeatedly at least another three or four times during the flight; having aborted all previous attempts, due to her continual nodding off halfway in to it. Following another lengthy snooze she checked the itinerary and was surprised that the journey to her first stop-off in Dubai would involve passing through Baghdad and Middle Eastern airspace. Little did she know at the time there had been pandemonium back home.

Grimm and Tia had been observing her flight online and for at least twenty minutes the plane has disappeared out of sight, as her plane flew over the Middle Eastern airspace. Grimm began to panic when he remembered the Malaysian Aircraft that had suddenly dropped out of the sky without trace a few weeks earlier. Until that moment he had been keeping Tia updated about the progress of the flight, but under the circumstances he decided to abstain from doing so, at least until her plane had been confirmed missing. The plane soon resurfaced again online having passed Baghdad and just eight hundred and sixty-four miles away from Dubai.

Her Father had always raved non-stop about his love for Dubai and his plans to live there in the future, however as the plane made its descent towards the concourse of the runway, she was unimpressed with the larger than life views on show from the sky. Anyone else in would have been overjoyed with the extremity of the architecture and waterfalls, but for her the fake landscapes and aesthetics were having the complete opposite effect. As she entered inside the airport the atmosphere inside, during the ungodly hours of the morning she had arrived did nothing to dispel her lack of affinity with the place. There were very few women around by the time she had arrived and the security attendants in customs appeared brash and heavy-handed with some of the passengers on her flight who had been waiting in line. It reminded her of a typical scene from the BBC's classic television series 'Tenko' set in the early 1940's as the custom officers continuously barked orders at them, "Take of your shoes" and "Empty your bag", seemed to be among the most frequent phrases being instructed and there was a definite lack of customer interaction or exchange on display. The distance to where she needed to board the next flight plane was at least a ten minute walk away; as she struggled to find her way, no notices were made available and the information boards had either not been updated or were displaying inaccurate information. She was not bothered by it too much and the other passengers who had also been on-board her flight appeared to stick out like a sore thumb in comparison to the natives of Dubai.

She was able to find a spare seat nearby some of the passengers on her flight, whilst she waited in the boarding area. It was the first chance she had since her arrival to take in the sights around the airport, she denoted it lacked lustre and a lot smaller than she had first imagined, considering the extravagant and outlandish views she had just witnessed outside the airport. As she boarded her flight to Brunei she felt a real sense of affinity with the country in complete contrast to her time spent in Dubai. The scenery during the descent appeared very green and beautiful, yet compact. She felt a sense of peace and serenity as the plane landed. She prepared herself for how small she had heard the airport was, and soon realised if she completed a full three-sixty degree twirl, she would be able to see the entire airport at a glance. The temperature inside the airport was like a furnace both London Heathrow and Dubai airport had been on the chilly side, which aided in preventing her from falling asleep. She felt she would struggle to remain awake in Brunei, she did not have the energy to even people watch and the more she tried to, the more tired she felt. There was a five and a half hour wait before she would be able to continue with the remaining part of her journey. With the time she had available she headed for the bathroom and decided on a long shower and took her time freshening up, hoping to pass the time away.

With a change of clothes and feeling refreshed she sat in the waiting area and looked through the airport window and studied the aircraft visible on the concourse she would be expecting to board later. Considering the size of the airport and the amount of people waiting, it was significantly quiet. She wandered over to the perfume counter of the small duty-free section they had and began spraying herself with the first perfume she liked Pacco Rabanne Lady Million. One of the sales attendants approached and handed her a bottle of Prada Pink Candy as an alternative scent to try and quickly doused herself all over with it. She had not been prepared for the random act of kindness she had been shown she began to feel a little more comfortable in the unfamiliar surroundings as she checked out the other facilities available within the airport. She popped in to the restaurant and coffee shop areas and made good use of her Darussalam Dollars from the various tourist stalls before returning to the waiting area. She felt conflicted between excitement and a need for more sleep, before finally settling on the former as she waited patiently for the few remaining minutes to pass before boarding the plane for the final part of the journey. She could barely contain her excitement as she stood near to the entrance for boarding, almost blocking the entrance for the priority passengers who were required to be seated ahead of her. On board she soon found her seat, made herself comfortable and loaded the film 'The Intern' before soon falling fast asleep.

She awoke abruptly during the Pilot's announcement sounding in her headphones, they had just entered Australia and there was another four hours of flying time to be completed before she touched down in sunny Melbourne. She thought she would burst she was that happy, to contain her excitement she dosed off for another couple of hours. She felt quite proud of herself too, it had been many years since she had travelled alone, but never so far that within itself was a major accomplishment for her. She popped into the WC on board the plane to freshen up; her twenty-five hour flight would be ending shortly. She literally couldn't wait to see Hita and knew the feeling would be mutual. Hita had arranged for Paul to meet her at the airport; she considered her relationship with Paul was quite close they had known each other for more than ten years and had developed a solid friendship. She got through customs quite quickly at Melbourne airport, unlike the images she had seen on the Australian border control television programs she was all too familiar with. The customs officer was fairly pleasant and discreet during their meeting, he welcomed her in to the country and stated as long as she completed the required declarations; she would be made to feel welcome whenever she visited. The baggage collection area was really busy with hordes of passengers waiting for their luggage to arrive. She could overhear the airport security staff barking instructions aimed at those travelers who had retrieved their luggage instructing them on the documentation they were required to have to hand, to complete the final process of immigration, before exiting the airport. Fortunately for her she was able to bypass that part of the process, upon collecting her suitcase she was waved through the exit of the airport by a lone security staff member.

She waited outside the airport and began taking in the sights, on first inspection she noticed how orderly and colourful it appeared in contrast to other it airports. It was eight in the morning on the Thursday she had arrived. It had just finished raining but the environment felt humid, giving the impression it had possibly been extremely warm the day before, either way it was remarkably warmer than the sub-zero temperatures she had left back in the UK. Paul arrived about fifteen minutes later recognizing her instantly, it had been a couple of years since they had last seen each other; on the contrary it wouldn't have been difficult for him to notice her as there were very few people waiting outside the airport who looked anything similar to her. By the time they had loaded the car and drove away from the airport, Paul immediately began to question her, mainly reiterating what he had previously been told by Hita. She briefly updated him about her split with Grimm; he appeared genuinely shocked by the news. Paul had gotten to know Grimm well and when she explained why the relationship had ended, she was surprised Paul by the support he offered her. His response pleased her and added to her feeling welcomed, little did she know that a few days thereafter the support Paul once offered her would be very much compromised and only time would tell whether the bond they shared would continue.

As they made their approach homeward bound Paul took the scenic route home, so he could give her a mini tour along the way. They passed by a block of apartments Hita had lived in when she first moved to Australia and another apartment they had bought together soon after meeting. He promised to take her back to the properties for a more detailed look during her stay. She was already impressed with what she had seen so far, the apartments overlooked the Yarra River, making them were sensible purchases and they were certain to retain their value, due to their location. Paul phoned Hita on the way to theirs and they spoke briefly, she experienced her first phone call with the now much older Nile. She couldn't believe how well versed he was. The last time she had seen Nile he was only six months old and very dependent on his Mother's breast milk, feeding on demand and quite grizzly without 'boob', as Hita referred to it. She could relate she had experienced the same with Tia breastfeeding on demand for almost two years. Nile was now three years old and they were having the biggest conversation. He was just as excited to see her as she was to see him. Although she had been speaking to Hita using her husband's phone, Hita refused to believe she was actually in Australia, until she was able to see her with her own eyes.

As they turned in to Sydney Avenue, based in the Emerald suburbs where they lived, Paul pointed out Hita's place of business Emerald Psychology Practice, they had recently opened. It was situated less than ten minutes away from where they lived. Paul hauled the car up the hill and parked in front of their residence instantly she noticed two things.   One was that the home already looked completely different from when it was first purchased and the improvements where obvious in comparison to the pictures she had sent when they had first bought it a couple of years before. The second thing was having witnessed the car climb a straight hill which seemed almost impossible, the hill was straight yet steep there was a part in the climb where you were unable to see the surface ahead, only the sky was visible for less than a couple of feet, she had not experienced anything like it and the drive to the top of it left her slightly unnerved. As soon as she had entered through the main sliding doors to the property, Hita waiting for her the two long lost friends embraced each other after being face to face again for the first time in almost three years. She quickly dropped her luggage and they embraced each other again. Appreciative of the time they had been apart, seemed to make the moment they reunited even more meaningful.

This was a giant milestone for her, over the past ten years she had tried extensively to make the journey to Australia on at least two previous occasions. The first time she had booked the flights she had ended up losing all her deposit, owing to being made redundant just two months thereafter. The second occasion she managed to book and lose all the money a second time due to a serious long-term illness she had unexpectedly developed which incurred her being off work for almost two years. She regretted what happened, but not as much as she regretted being unable to attend their wedding. Her attendance had been confirmed and at the last minute, she had to pull out and missed the opportunity of being present at her best friend's wedding in Sibu Island, Maylasia. She had been made redundant again with the added responsibility of being the main breadwinner in the family meant; she had been unable to prioritize the wedding ahead of her own circumstances, the decision not to attend did not sit well with her, but it was outside of her control. Hita whilst saddened by the prospect understood her dilemma, but she had problems forgiving herself for not being present on one of the most important days of both their lives. As a result, she felt guilty and labelled herself a bad friend to Hita especially when she had always been so good to her. The setback had a profound effect on her and she promised herself from then on whenever she made arrangements with Hita she would ensure to keep to them, no matter what.

During the middle of the pleasantries regarding the flight and the lengthy journey she had completed, a tiny little voice interrupted them mid-conversation "Is that you Auntie?" Nile said whilst dangling from the bottom of the stairs of the main entry. All of their attention instantly diverted towards where Nile, she moved from where they had been standing and immediately made her way over to him confirming it was her. Nile had grown so much since she had last seen him at six months, donning a white baby-grow at the time. Three years later Nile was a whole complete small person full of character, now walking and speaking in full sentences, unaided and with oodles of self-confidence, it was as if he had known 'Auntie' all his life. Hita suggest she have a shower to make herself comfortable, and told her she had a surprise for her that she would reveal after. She wondered what the surprise could possibly be and quickly showered, Hita knew she hated surprises and struggled with kind gestures. She threw on some shorts and an oversized t-shirt and made her way up to the living room where they were waiting for her. She couldn't help but be in awe of her surroundings; the photographic memorabilia fixed on almost every wall space provided a full documentary of Hita's time in Australia since she had moved there. As she made her way to the living room, Paul and Hita had a massive 'I know something you don't know look', about them.   She waited with baited breath, deep down a little daunted whilst petering on the verge of concern, she was worried she was being drafted into something she might not be so comfortable doing.

Hita explained that prior to her arriving in Australia; she had decided not to go on the annual fishing trip that year, due to having the little ones to look after and had decided it would be too much for her to manage. However, now that she was there it had been all confirmed and the surprise they had arranged for was them to all go away camping for three nights the following day. Deep down she hated the idea, not only had she never been camping before, she considered the activity way outside her remit. Grimm had tried to convince her to go camping during their entire relationship and had been completely unsuccessful in his efforts. She smiled broadly and explained she had never done it before and really didn't think she would be able to participate. Hita reassured her that it was not as bad as it sounded and that the typical British camping, congruent to a Glastonbury event Grimm had often mentioned; she had done before to her astonishment and that she would never do it again. She felt assured Hita would not syphon her off for an adventure she wanted no part of. She began to think of Grimm and thought that maybe he would have been better off performing this activity, rather than her. Fishing although not his favourite activity; she knew it was something that he was better suited to do, as opposed to how far removed it was from anything she would be inclined to do. She knew upon her return to the UK both Tia and Grimm would deem this part of her adventure particularly entertaining when they heard it.

***

The morning of the camping excursion she awoke early enough to get ready and make herself available to assist with any childcare duties that might be needed, she would stick to this format, in order to be of little burden as possible during her stay. Together they loaded the car with the necessary essentials, whilst Paul attached a small trailer that contained the camping equipment on to the rear of his four by four vehicle they set off. She was seated perfectly in between the two boys on the back seat; it would allow her the much needed quality time she desired in getting to know them both, Paul and Hita were positioned in the front of the vehicle and would appreciate the break as they navigated their way to the required destination.   The first pit stop was less than fifteen minutes in to the drive they stopped at a local bakery that sold the infamous Australian meat pies.   Due to it being still ridiculously early in the morning, she did not fancy having one at that time of the day; she was still full from the meal Hita had made the night before. The small bakery had an overly extended menu of delights to choose from, before she settled on a spinach and ricotta pasty that she found very tasty.

They arrived at McGauran's beach approximately three hours later; it was such a beautiful day the temperature was very warm with a cloudless blue sky that covered the deserted ninety mile beach. The view alone was picturesque and completely tranquil, the only time she recalled seeing scenery such as this was on a postcard or professional photo. Hita's in-laws Spud and Pat and a few of their friends from the fishing club had already arrived and were busily either setting up camp or partaking in a few beers seated outside. She was quickly introduced to the other campers present and made to feel very welcome. Hita and Paul began unloading the supplies from the vehicle whilst Bernadette escorted her over the bank and on to the beach and for the first time since she had arrived she was able to witness the breathtaking view in its full glory. The views in front of her were just simply amazing, the deep blue sea was calm and inviting and the sand beneath her was warm to the touch, it even glistened from the penetration of the sun. The wind had a gentle breeze to it, ideal for the ninety six degree heat that accompanied it. Bernadette talked about her travels with her brother to the UK; she had visited a few times and really enjoyed it there. She humored she often travelled with her brother and would invite herself along and by doing so she had been able to bag other free trips to Europe with him. Bernadette had travelled extensively and nearly had all the Air Mile points she needed, for the round-the-world trip she planned on treating herself to.

As they made their way back to the secluded campsite, most of the other campers had finished setting up and were seated outside socialising, she helped Paul set up their tents, whilst Hita tended to the babies. Spud and Pat's caravan had originally been a bus, Spud had spent several years refurbishing it into a mobile caravan complete with a double bed, full kitchen, shower and utility room, TV, fridge freezer, microwave and a whole host of other adaptions that would be able to compete with any new age modern motor available on the market. The caravan was so impressive Paul bragged that when the time came for his parents' property to be divided amongst his siblings, the only item he wanted was the caravan. Paul had no interest in any other property, money or assets his parents owned. Whilst the campers conversed, there was mention of the others they were still expecting to arrive. She overheard that Danny had decided not to attend, due to some personal issues with his ex-girlfriend Margaret. They had ended the relationship the day she arrived in Melbourne. The breakup had been a volatile one. Margaret partially blamed Hita for the demise in the relationship having discovered Hita had been more supportive of Danny than her. Margaret believed Hita had over stepped the mark and sent her a lengthy abusive text message detailing how she felt. She explained in no uncertain terms what she now thought of her and further dissolved their friendship by aptly blocking her on all social media platforms. Hita was gutted with the loss of the friendship and received very little sympathy from either her or Paul who had both warned her to stay previously to stay out of their affairs altogether.

Brett, a close friend and ex-colleague of Paul's had mentioned he was hoping his friend Robbo would also attend. He had expected him to arrive that day; however Robbo had since made contact and it looked unlikely he would be able to make it. Pat mentioned that there were other members from the fishing group that would be arriving later that day and the day after. As she began to settle in with the group, she felt slightly unnerved that there were others expected to arrive that she had not met before. She hoped they would like her as much as the other campers appeared to. Pat had made lunch for them consisting of sandwiches, cake, beer and pear cider. She began to absorb the views around her and as she did so it dawned on her, for the first time in a long while she began to feel as if she was actually living, only forty-eight hours ago her life had seemed so bleak and here she was just two days later, laughing and enjoying herself as if she didn't have a care in the world, finally experiencing some inner peace.

The following morning she was up at seven, considering it was her first time sleeping in a tent she had slept particularly well, although she still remained a little fatigued she put it down to jet lag as well as the nineteen beers and apple cider she had managed to consume during the course of the previous day. She had not gone to bed until the early hours of the morning, with her section of the dual tent unzipped, being careful not to disturb the others, she ventured outside to brush her teeth and have a strip wash whilst the other campers continued sleeping. The sun and blue skies were as perfectly formed as they had been the day before. She had a quick glance around the camp site and decided to change into the designer shorts Tia had customized for her and an opened-back casual t-shirt. Determined to acquire an all even tan, her weather app showed it was set to be a glorious ninety-eight degrees. Once she had dressed she exited the tent, there was little for her to do as they had tidied the camp area the night before. Nile was awake and began the morning moaning, desperately needing attention from his Mum. Spud was up early and dressed, they greeted each other whilst he put the kettle on. He was keen to get the day started and began preparing a cooked breakfast so he could first to go fishing. With breakfast underway, others from the group began to surface, some of the campers were hungover and struggling to get it together, due to their antics the night before. She found it slightly amusing as they all surfaced to the seating area to discuss either their plans of fishing for the day or revived drunken tales from the night before. She had been seated facing the sun now she could feel the heat of it directed on to her exposed legs slathered in sheer butter and sun protector, she couldn't believe how hot they felt, considering it was still fairly early in the day.

Brett being one of the last to arise had decided not to join the others due to being one of the last to have gone to bed the first night. He had gotten inebriated the night before and had ended up providing the campers with most of the entertainment. She felt particularly fond of Brett, he had observed her shivering when it got brisk during the night and kindly lent her his windproof camouflage jacket. She was so grateful and impressed by his kindness towards her. Initially she had only planned to borrow the jacket just for the night, but it had served its purpose so well in keeping her warm and snug she had slept in it. She thanked Brett again for the loan of the jacket and established he would be staying the entire time she was there and she chose to hold on to the jacket until she left the campsite. She offered to have the jacket professionally cleaned after using it, Brett found her suggestion amusing and informed her that would not be necessary.

At lunchtime another four by four pulled up and parked next to Brett's caravan, she had not seen the driver of the vehicle until Brett introduced them. Robbo was a very close friend of Brett's as well as an ex-colleague of Paul's and Hita's. She quickly ascertained Robbo was the friend Brett had been referring to the day before. Her first impression of Robbo was similar to her impression of Brett when she was first introduced to him, as he came over to shake her hand. She thought they both looked alike and appeared to be similar in nature; Brett and Robbo appeared to be the best of friends and seemed to have a lot in common, gambling, reading the newspaper and drinking beer. With the sun now at its peak they all sat together, now and again she would glance over at Brett and Rob and remark to herself how uncanny their similarities were from where she was seated they appeared almost identical they were sat in the same position and even dressed the same, donning straw hats, singlets, shorts and flip-flops. They reminded her of the stereotypical Aussie images of men you would find in a Fosters beer advertising campaign accompanied by their broad Australian accents. It was comical to her, but she kept her thoughts to herself ensuring she did not offend anyone with her evaluation of them.

She had not notice Rob leave his seat to get some more beer, she had been distracted with Nile as he conversed with Paul and her about his latest adventure on the beach, whilst she listened to Nile avidly, she suddenly jumped up in surprise due to the impact of the cold can of beer Rob had placed on the back of her neck, as he returned to his seat to join them. She laughed the prank off; it had been so unexpected she wasn't quite sure what to make of the gesture. Immediately after the initial impact had worn off, she had felt quite grateful to Rob the contact from the can of beer placed on the back of her neck had instantly helped her to cool down and offered some temporary relief from the heat of the sun. She took Rob's prank as a sign he was accepting of her being in his company. An hour later whilst still seated next to Paul, he informed her that he had asked Rob to bring her something 'special', she did not believe Paul at first but she was delighted upon hearing it all the same. She gave Paul a big hug and double-checked he wasn't pulling her leg. She looked over towards where Rob had been seated, but he was no longer there, as she turned to check where he might have gone to, she felt it again. Rob had managed to place yet another ice cold can of beer down the back of her neck without her even seeing him leave his seat, she inwardly hoped Rob would not consider her a worthy subject of his pranks the whole time they were there. Another couple not previously known to the group had also joined the camp site; they introduced themselves to the others and joined them accompanied with homemade buttered scones to the delight of the other campers.

Rob helped himself to one of the scones they had been given and began distributing the remaining scones to the other campers, he offered her one from the batch, but whenever she attempted to pick one he teasingly removed the tin from her grasp and held it close to him, preventing her from choosing from the selection. After a couple of attempts of him doing so she stopped him midway and mentioned, the 'special item' he had brought for her and that she looked forward to sampling it later. Rob confirmed he had brought something special with him for her and invited her to try it with him later that afternoon. She felt overwhelmed at the efforts these strangers were making for her, it brought on a sense of humility and she began to reflect on the kindness she had been shown since she had been there. Within the first minutes of meeting Pat she had gifted her with a pair of sunglasses, due to forgetting her own.

Later that afternoon Rob suggested they go for a walk along the beach to sample the 'surprise' reefer he had brought for them. As they walked over to his vehicle, he explained how he had acquired it and she was most impressed with his efforts. Surprisingly she felt quite relaxed with Rob they had a natural unison as if they had known each other many years. Rob asked her to build the reefer and told her he was not very good at making them. She explained that she was probably just as bad at it and hoped her efforts would not disappoint. With the reefer prepared they made their way past the other campers; she wondered if anyone thought despondently about them wandering off together so soon after meeting. Only a few of the campers knew what they were up to and she quickly dispelled the negative thoughts. They made their way over to what looked like the perfect spot to sample it, there was a small dip in the bank slightly hidden out of view, the dip in the bank was only large enough for them to sit side by side and almost hidden from view. Rob lit the reefer from what she could tell it smelt amazingly strong. Rob pulled on it a couple of times and passed it over to her she inhaled it in a little, but enough to feel the strong effects of the smoke she had inhaled. She liked it a lot and pulled on it again, she honestly felt it was the best she had ever had and shared her findings with Rob. He seemed pleased with the feedback as she offered it back to him. He told her some more about the origins it, whilst they finished the rest of it she told him about her experiences in sampling around the various countries she had travelled, but had not expected to try it there. It reminded her of what was available in Amsterdam as opposed to any other she had visited. She was certainly impressed with the quality of what Rob had and quickly concluded he was a connoisseur of sorts. With the reefer finished she suggested they make their way back to the campsite, but first she wanted to dip her feet in the sea before they headed back. This would soon form part of a ritual every time they went for an adult smoke.

Back at the camp site it was evident to the entire group what they had been up to, Paul had updated them about their whereabouts and what they had been up to during the time they had left. They reacquainted themselves with the others back at the camp site, whilst childishly being teased by the other members of the group, implying there was more to their stroll together. Paul asked her whether the reefer had been any good, she confirmed it definitely had been and again thanked him for organising it for her. Whilst the group chit-chatting Rob ventured over to his vehicle and began putting two fishing rods together, he grabbed a bucket and headed towards the bank as he walked past the other campers he yelled out to them he was off fishing. Paul initiated concern once Rob was out of sight and stated Rob had left to fish without taking any bait. She instantly felt guilty and spoke to Paul about his concerns, she became further worried when Paul stated that Rob had not smoked in over ten years. Feeling growingly concerned she spoke to Brett and informed him about what Paul had said. Rob hadn't mentioned any of this to her, the potency of the reefer was so strong she was concerned Rob had become overly affected by it and worried for him. Brett understood her concerns and devised a plan that involved them casually checking in on Rob and coaxing him back to camp site by suggesting that tea was ready.

Ten minutes later Brett accompanied her to locate Rob, as they made their way up to the top of the bank; she was relieved to see Rob in the far distance casting a fishing rod out to sea. She quickly dispelled any concerns she may have had earlier. Rob seemed pretty pleased that they had both come to see how he was; he assured them he was okay and had wanted to test the water for fishing. He said he would give it another ten mins or so before heading back to and asked her if she would stay and keep him company. She agreed to his suggestion whilst Brett left them and returned to the other campers. Rob assured her he was having a good time and was particularly enjoying her company. Having been in a relationship for the past seven years, she didn't think any more of it and stated she was enjoying herself just as much and so far it was a lot better from her usual routine back home. They made their way back to the camp site soon after and in time for tea, having had no success fishing. She insisted on clearing the dishes after the group had eaten, she didn't think she had any other skills that would be useful to the campsite. As the evening drew nearer they prepared to settle down for the evening. A camp fire was built and the deck chairs were placed within a large circle around it.

Rob invited her to join him for a smoke and she eagerly accepted, as they heading over to the bank they were ribbed again by some of the members of the group, she laughed it off no longer embarrassed, knowing they were all aware of what they were up to. They returned to the dip in the sand and Rob lit the reefer, this time the conversation between them became a little more intense. Rob seemed eager to find out more about her. He asked her how long she was planning to be in Australia and enquired about her family back in London, but she felt a little skeptical when he asked her about her relationship status. She confirmed she would be leaving Australia in a couple of weeks and that her visit had been a spur of the moment decision. She informed told him she had a daughter named Tia, and briefly mentioned her recent split with Grimm and that she needed a break from it all and mentioned she hadn't been happy in the relationship for at least four years prior to separating from her partner. Rob explained that he had two grown up daughters and that he had been married for over thirty years. She was shocked when he had first mentioned it, until then she didn't think he looked old enough to have two grown up daughters in their late twenties and certainly didn't appear the type to have been in a committed marriage for as long as thirty years. Rob explained that whilst he was married, the marriage had not been good for the past four years and whilst he was saddened the state of his marriage had declined, his biggest issue was the negative treatment he received from his wife and they only continued with the marriage just for the sake of it.

As she listened intently to him she sympathised with how downcast he has feeling, particularly regarding the rejection and hurt he presented, as Rob described the problems within his marriage and discussed how the relationship had fallen apart. She was still coming to terms with the former information he had already told her earlier regarding the events leading up to the troubled marriage. She asked him his age and was sidelined by his response, he informed her he was fifty-five years of age and she confirmed she was forty-four when he enquired. For a moment she felt as if the sail had been taken out from beneath her, the more she discovered about him, the more she was able to identify she was amazed by the similarities they shared regarding their life experiences. With the reefer finished, she became conscious of the length of time they had been away from the others. She suggested they ought to head back to the campsite, once they had dipped their feet in the sea. She also thanked him for the talk and that she found it uncanny, how two people from opposite sides of the world could share so much in common. Although Rob loved and cared for his wife, he admitted the passion within the marriage had died and he was no longer able to prevent the inevitable. She asked him what he planned to do about the state of the marriage, and enquired whether they had tried to salvage it with counselling. Rob confirmed he had tried, but his wife had refused to attend the sessions even though he still attended counselling sessions alone, he deemed the experience for his wife unsuccessful.

Rob was uncertain about what he wanted to do next, but maintained something needed to be done. Rob further shocked her when out of nowhere he randomly asked her for a kiss. She was completely taken aback by his suggestion that she had not seen coming and respectfully as she could manage, politely declined the unwarranted gesture. Rob asked her to explain why she had refused him and she explained obviously because of what he had just informed her of pertaining to his marriage and she reminded him she had only recently ended a long-term relationship. She considered herself worthier than a holiday fling, Rob told her he understood her decision and apologised for his outburst. On their way back to the campsite Rob informed her that he found her very attractive and felt they had a lot in common, although she agreed there were things they had in common, she felt strongly that there would be nothing else between them other than friendship. Rob respected her decision, by the time they had dipped their feet in the water and began making their way back to join the others; Rob had reached for her hand and held on to it firmly. She looked over at him enquiringly, Rob told her that it felt natural holding her hand and that he loved that they were able to be open and honest with each other. They walked back up the bank hand in hand, prior to being detected by the others. Back at the camp site the atmosphere appeared to be in full swing, Hita had been waiting for her to return and had worried about the time she had been missing with Rob. She reassured her she was fine, Hita had been waiting for her to return because she wanted to turn in early after putting the babies to bed. She agreed with her decision to have an early night and offered to help with the children. Hita refused the offer immediately and suggested she remain with the others and enjoy herself. With Hita and the boys in bed she returned to the group and sat beside Paul and Brett in front of the camp fire.

Rob left momentarily to source a deck chair and positioned it next to hers; he told her again that he had really enjoyed her company earlier and that he was glad he had made the effort to come on the trip. He stated his pleasure of having met her and thanked her for taking the time to listen to him discuss his marriage. Spud later joined them and showed photos of his upcoming holiday. She swapped seats with Spud so the other group members could get a better view. Rob was not happy with her decision to swap seats with Spud and he whispered to her "Please stay seated next to me." She told him she felt it was the right thing to do by and that she would return to her seat as soon as Spud was finished. Rob seemed saddened by her response and spent the time they were seated apart staring at her intently until she returned.

As Dusk approached, the group showed no signs of settling down. Rob suggested they head off for a smoke, but it was so dark she said she did not fancy venturing out as far as the bank they usually frequented. Rob agreed with her and suggested they found somewhere nearer, they ventured over to his vehicle and made the smoke, Paul and Brett who were considerably drunk joined them. Paul tried to convince Brett they should go off to the adjoining paddock to hunt Kangaroos; Brett attempted to explain why he felt it was a bad idea and Rob did his best to intervene, reminding Paul of the consequences should his wife find out. Paul persisted and eventually convinced Brett to join him. Within ten minutes they had returned, it was pitch black by the time they had left, the hunt was abandoned shortly thereafter due to the unsuitable conditions.

During their absence Rob attempted to make the most of the time they had together and cheekily asked her for a hug, she agreed and tapped him fondly on the back as she did so. Paul had seen their embrace and raced over as he drunkenly slurred, "What is going on?" They both burst out laughing in response and guiltily replied "Nothing." They had innocently been saying goodnight before retiring for bed. With no harm done, Paul made his excuses and announced he was off to bed, she also felt inclined to turn in for the night. Most of the others had either left the campsite or were thinking of turning in for the night, leaving just three of the newcomers still seated around the camp fire. It had been a particularly windy night and she was finding it difficult to sleep as the wind howled persistently. Considering how late it was, she made time to mull over the events of the day. She thought about Rob and the things he had told her, she was eager to go back outside and continue where they had left off, but thought better of it as she drifted off to sleep.

She was up early the next day, she felt a little groggy yet excited to begin the day, she looked forward to seeing Rob and being in his company again. As she peered in to the campsite after leaving the tent, she began tidying up the few discarded items that were strewn around. Spud joined her soon after and offered to make breakfast for them both, she insisted on helping, but Spud would not hear of it, motioned for her to take a seat and she gratefully accepted. Just before Spud had finished breakfast Rob put in an appearance and sat next to her with a cupper in tow. He confirmed he had enjoyed the night and they reminisced over the events that occurred.

With breakfast finished Spud left them to go fishing, the other fishermen joined him and ended up spending much of the day competing, eager to catch the largest fish and scoop the winning prize, ahead of the competition deadline the following day. Carley the youngest member of the group was only ten had never fished before joining them at the campsite and had practically shut down the entire fishing competition. She had quickly realized she had the knack for catching fish every time she went fishing. The fish just seemed to gravitate towards her bucket like a magnet. She caught more fish than anyone else in the entire the group. The other fishermen began to notice how good Carley was, some fisherman keen to not be outdone by her, resorted to tactical methods and cast out Drones over the sea, hopeful to increase their chances, but none of their tactics had any effect on Carley's efforts.

The ladies within the group spent the day sat around conversing whilst catching a few rays and indulging in a few bevvies, she joined the others and topped her tan as this would be their final full day. She had overheard a few of the couples discussing leaving the campsite a day early, if they were unsuccessful with the fishing. As she listened to the others, her mind soon drifted off and mainly settled on what had transpired the night before with Rob and thought about her family back home. She wondered how her Tia was coping without her, whilst she had been at the camp site there had been no signal on her mobile phone. Her daughter knew that she had gone to a remote area with no opportunity to have a mobile phone conversation back home. Hita noticed her friend had become quiet and deep in thought and she asked her, if she was okay. She remarked she was having the time of her life and could remain at McGauran's Beach forever and that she would always remember the experience. Hita then surprised her with an offer she had had only ever mentioned twice during their friendship. "Why don't you come out here and hang with me for twelve months?" She couldn't believe what she was hearing. She looked up at Hita with tears in her eyes and replied "Really, Heets. Are you sure?" Hita replied. "Don't be silly, I'd love for you to stay for twelve months, and then if you really like it here you could consider staying on a permanent basis." She really couldn't get her head around what Hita was asking of her or the opportunity she was being offered. She thought about their friendship, as a friend especially in recent times she felt she had not been there for Hita in the way she thought she ought to have been. The fact that Hita would still be offering her this opportunity ten years later was baffling to her.

She constantly felt guilty about not visiting before now, Hita had made it easy for her coming to visit her in the UK almost yearly. Over the past three years it had only been due to the children being so young, that prevented her from travelling. "If you're really sure Hita I would love to," as she reached out to show her gratitude. She made a point of thanking her for the opportunity once again, trying her best to hold it together. She remained in complete shock that this opportunity had presented itself again after all these years. She realized that in a matter of just three days of being in Australia, her life was going to change drastically and for the better. She had instantly found a renewed focus and could not wait to return to the UK to start organising things at home for when she returned. There was now so much to sort out and with a new spring in her step she was raring to go. Pat had made lunch for Spud and the other fishermen and took it down to them, whilst they returned to their conversation of fine tuning the details of her return to Australia.

By the late afternoon those that had been fishing began returning to the camp, after weighing the fish they had caught that morning, it turned out to be the largest catch of the day since they had been at the campsite. It was decided they would start the camp fire early after dinner, being the last night they would be staying there. The majority of campers planned to leave first thing in the morning.

Another couple she had not met yet had also arrived at the campsite, they turned out to be as friendly as the others camp members and invested a lot of time getting to know her. She encouraged Hita to retire early for the night, having exhausted herself with the demands of looking after the children. She wondered how she coped with it all. She was still recovering from having Ashton and the 'snap-back' had taken a little longer than she had anticipated, she had been left with a large unsightly hole in her stomach after the birth and it was taking it's time to heal. Hits had been made to wear a special bandage to encourage the healing process for six months, with a view to having an operation to seal the hole if there were no improvement by then. All the same, Hita still remained as beautiful as ever and Motherhood very much suited her. They had come a long way over the years, and her life just oozed success with every decision she made to improve her future. Hita's life stood as a testimony that the reward for working hard meant you were in control of your own destiny. Hita made it look effortless and only those who were there from the beginning knew of the challenges she had faced to achieve the lifestyle she now had.

On the surface she made it look easy, however Paul although a good father for the boys did not work and hadn't done so for several years. Paul was in the middle of an employment dispute with his former employer that had occurred almost five years prior and had been holding out for a compensation payout, believing he had been the victim. The case had been to court and there had been endless mediation sessions conducted over the years with very little sign of a resolution offered between the opposing parties. Paul had not bothered to seek alternative employment and instead enjoyed the proceeds from his wife's business. This meant that the total financial family income rested entirely on his wife. Paul also had a reputation for being lazy and she felt there were times he would use the boys as an excuse for not having to work. Hita turned a blind eye to Paul's unemployment, yet appeared to be worn out from all the extra responsibility she was undertaking.

With the early evening drawing near the group sat seated around the fire, Pat complained the fishing competition would be ending tomorrow and thought it was embarrassing that a child, who wasn't even a member of the fishing team was likely to win the competition; although Pat had a valid point, the way she presented her findings to the group was quite comical, the entire group roared with laughter in response to her. Bernadette sided with Pat and with a look of determination they stood up from their seats, collected their fishing rods and walked over the bank together, hoping to change the outcome of the competition results. An hour later Spud wondered whether his wife had managed to catch any fish, she offered to go and out and check on them for him, before leaving the group Spud passed her a jacket for Pat as the weather picked up a chill. She made her way over the bank towards them and caught Pat and Bernadette celebrating the Trout they had each just caught. She returned to the campsite and updated Spud and the others. Pat and Bernadette returned a while later having caught a few more. Rob later told her he had missed her during the time she had been away. They reminisced over the new nickname he had chosen for her 'Shaga' with the time she found to sunbathe she had developed somewhat of a two-toned tan on her thighs, the camp had found her tanned stripes quite amusing and Spud had amended the new nickname Rob had given her to 'Two-Toned Shaga'. Rob was saddened that they would be leaving the next day and although they had only just met, he wanted them to remain in contact and hoped they'd meet up again prior to her return to London. They exchanged contact details and promised to keep in touch. The group stayed up until at least three in the morning, with some staying awake even later. They had all enjoyed their time together and the memories they shared.

The following morning most of the group had awoken early in preparation for an early departure. She was already dressed and packed by the time most of others began venturing outside of their tents. She sat on one of the chairs that had been placed around the camp fire from the night before. Spud had kindly offered to make her one of his infamous breakfast rolls, whilst she warmed her hands and enjoyed a cupper. Rob soon appeared and exited Brett's caravan, he immediately made his way over to her and they resonated about the end of their adventure and reminisced over the events from the night before, wishing they had a few more days longer. Rob was keen to make future arrangements and they agreed that when she left Australia, they would meet up en route to the airport and spend at least an hour together prior to catching her flight.

They went for a final stroll over the bank and walked along the beach. They confessed that they would miss each other's company, considering the short time they had gotten to know each other. Rob stated it was refreshing to meet someone who he felt he could build a genuine friendship with. By the time they had returned to the campsite all the other campers had left with only Hita, Paul and their family remaining. Rob walked over to his vehicle and finished packing. Hita and Paul rushed over to her and demanded answers about what had been going on between them. She was initially surprised by the barrage of questions and maintained nothing had occurred and certainly not in the way they were implying. Apart from having a couple of smokes together, nothing more had transpired between them. She began to feel guilty about how the others may have misinterpreted the friendship between them.

Hita and Paul had concerns that since Rob's arrival they had become inseparable, she disagreed profusely with what they were suggesting and could not decide they were over-reacting or just generally winding her up. To further dispel their concerns she conceded herself far too old to be entertaining any thoughts of a holiday romance, which seemed to settle their opinions. Hita at least knew a holiday romance was not an option for her and would only result in more heartache. Since her arrival she had shown little sign that she was still dealing with the effects of the break up. Rob popped over to see her before setting off to wish her and the others farewell. They hugged each other and she remarked how lovely he smelt, he looked at her disbelievingly and she confirmed she absolutely loved his scent. He used the compliment she had given him as an opportune moment to ask her for a kiss. Feeling a little put on the spot she responded to his request and quickly pecked him on the lips discreetly as she did so, she asked herself what harm would it do, although Rob seemed keen on making plans to meet again, she had her doubts it would ever happen.

Immediately after the kiss she realized she suddenly felt differently about Rob, there was something there she hadn't felt until then. Apart from the kiss, she had a feeling they had unfinished business. She assessed it was possible she felt like this having not been kissed for the past four years. Rob left the campsite promising to remain in contact during her stay and looked forward to seeing her again as they had planned. Unknowingly to her Rob who was still taken aback by the compliment she had paid him, decided to wait at the nearest service station. He hoped Paul would drive the route where he was waiting and waited almost two hours for them to drive by, but had been no sign of them. He ascertained they had taken another route before driving away from the location. Rob had planned to stop the vehicle with any sighting of them and take her away for a coffee, so they could just talk and spend some time together just the two of them. Rob was disappointed that it had been a missed and called her instead.

***

The following day Hita and the family took her to Fountain Gate Shopping Centre in Melbourne, they had plans to take her for a spot of sightseeing in Melbourne Town center, including revisiting the riverside properties Paul had mentioned when she had first arrived, after which Hita and Paul would take her on a historical journey of their life together.   First they visited their preferred Chinese restaurant where she was able to sample their favourite dish. Whilst they were out Rob called her throughout the day and later Hita and Paul overheard him admit he was in love with her, realizing she felt the same as he did she stated how she felt. With the phone call over, she hoped Paul and Hita had not overheard them declaring their feelings for one another, but they had and appeared genuinely happy for her.   They were eager to learn all the details of how the relationship was progressing. She promised she would keep them updated, but only with any poignant moments. They convinced her that they were interested to know all the details, more than what she may be willing to disclose.   However her relationship with Rob was still in its very early stages and whilst she was excited about it, she felt a little unsure about how things would work out between them. One thing she felt certain of was that this would not become a holiday romance; she despised the idea and would ensure Rob was aware of how she felt when she saw him again.

They continued to speak daily, sometimes several times a day and whenever her mobile lost its connection she would speak to him via Paul's mobile. Rob admitted that she was constantly on his mind and he was really excited about seeing her again. She agreed that she found it difficult to think of anything else either, due to the constant contact they had as well as Hita and Paul constantly humouring her about the relationship whenever their calls ended. A few days later she received a weird call from Rob, he had decided that meeting up for an hour before she was due to leave for the UK would not suffice. Rob had taken the following day off work so they could spend the day together. Rob had sounded so sincere and desperate to see her, something she had not experienced in a relationship before. She updated Hita and Paul about Rob's intentions; they had lots of questions about Rob's reasons for changing the original plans, but she was as clueless as they were, she was eager to see him again, but she worried he might have a change of heart when he finally saw her again outside of the campsite setting.

Early the next morning with very little sleep the night before, all she could think of was Rob's impending visit. With the sudden change of plans she had no idea what she would wear and later settled on a demur black dress she had only worn on one occasion before. She begun to feel nervous Rob was due at any moment, she popped upstairs to find Hita. Hita looked drained and was busy feeding the baby, before she was able to ask, Hita told her she looked lovely. She offered to help with anything Hita needed doing before she left for the day, or would she rather her stay to help her out with the children, Hita would not hear of her cancelling her plans and stated the only thing Hita really wanted was her bed and there was nothing she could do to help with that. She told Hita about Rob's plans to leave home at the usual time that he would usually leave to avoid being detected. He had contacted his boss and informed him that he had an urgent personal matter to attend to and as a result he had been given the day off. He would then drive two hours to where Hita and Paul live in the middle of her update, they both heard Rob's vehicle pull up to the driveway. She nervously gave herself a quick once over and went downstairs to unlock the patio doors.

Rob was stood outside his truck as she approached him; he looked at her up and down intently, she reached out to hold him and whilst he reciprocated her embrace, he mumbled something about not being sure if he had awoken the others and that he had been waiting outside for ages. He was dressed in his work uniform and asked for somewhere to change in to something more suitable she took his hand and they entered inside. She led him in to her bedroom and told him to make himself comfortable, whilst she left the room momentarily to give him some privacy. Once he had changed they popped upstairs to see Hita and Paul before leaving. It was still very early in the morning and not an ideal time for house guests, they kept it brief and left, promising to return later that evening to cook the Jerk Chicken she had promised Paul.

Rob drove towards Emerald Main Town Centre he told her he was happy to see her again and she replied she felt the same. They decided to get some breakfast and then devise a plan of how they would spend the rest of the day together. Rob admitted he had not made any plans past them meeting up, but knew he wanted them to spend the day together and patted her thigh to further reassure. It had begun to drizzle and the sky was overcast, they ventured in to the nearest opened café they saw and ordered breakfast. They were so excited about what the day would bring, yet nervous being on their first official date. She ordered pancakes with syrup and a coffee, Rob also ordered a coffee and scrambled eggs on toast, whilst they waited for their orders, Rob talked about the café he had previously owned before selling it on, stating it was too much hard work with little reward and he had no longer enjoyed the responsibility that came with the ownership of having it.

After eating they argued about her insistence on paying for their meals, she felt it was the least she could do, after all the effort he had made to see her. Whilst they waited in the queue to pay, she became distracted by two young girls no more than ten years who had been looking over at them the entire time they had been there. She was intrigued with what they were discussing as they seemed particularly focused on her. She confronted them in jest and asked them directly if they were talking about her, surprised by her impertinence they quickly shot down her claims and appeared embarrassed by the confrontation. It was all harmless fun in her opinion; they paid the bill and left the café hand in hand and returned to the truck narrowly avoiding the heavy downpour. They both felt relaxed in each other's company, Rob decided they should book a room for the night and so they drove around calling in at various hotels and Inns trying to find somewhere last minute that might be able to accommodate them, it ended up being quite a comical situation as neither of them were familiar with the area they were in.

After endlessly driving around and with little luck they found a place and although it was full, the owner gave them the number for another establishment nearby. It took them a while to find the place, but eventually they did and were informed there was one remaining cottage available. The cottage was in the process of being cleaned, they were asked to return in twenty minutes, where they would be able to meet with the housekeeper and take a look at the property around before confirming whether they wanted it. They could not believe their eyes when they returned to view it. It happened to be one of the nicest cottages they had ever seen, and for the price they conceded it was certainly worth it. The entire cottage had a white and teal interior throughout, including a four poster bed, spa bath and shower en-suite, a fully furnished living room, fitted kitchen, a back yard, veranda and barbecue pit and to top it off the owner had given them a hamper full of food supplies. Having dropped their luggage off, Rob decided they should stop off at the local shops for some nibbles they could enjoy later. They had decided on a late lunch, Rob set up the barbecue and placed some of the food items on it from the hamper; together they cooked a fried breakfast. For a moment she felt incredibly shy whilst they ate their first meal together Rob also seemed nervous, however this was short lived as they conversed and got to know each other better.

After they had eaten Rob suggested they retire to the bedroom, where they made love for the first time. They both agreed the intimacy between them was special and they had not been prepared for the strong feelings they now held towards one another. This would be the last time she would see him before she left Australia, it made her emotional at the very thought of them having to say goodbye. Later that evening they returned to Hita's, whilst they had been gone, Hita's in-laws had visited to sample the infamous Jerk Chicken Paul had been constantly raving about. She was amazed at the way Rob appeared so relaxed under the circumstances, she quickly completed the pleasantries with Hita's in-laws, feeling slightly awkward she busied herself in the kitchen, hoping to get the jerk chicken underway and quickly eaten so they could leave and spend the rest of the time they had left together.

With the meal simmering away on the hob as they waited for it to finish cooking, she felt uncomfortable about returning to the living room where Hita and her Mother in-law were now seated. In the past Hita had confided in her about Pat being overly opinionated, to avoid any unwanted criticisms she remained in the kitchen clearing away the utensils and tidying the kitchen. Paul popped in to check on her and find out how long before the meal would be ready. They laughed together about their infused version of the jerk chicken she made. Hita and Paul had a ceiling to floor cupboard dedicated to every kind of seasoning imaginable; however they did not have jerk seasoning. They had searched everywhere for it but to no avail, in the end they admitted defeat and she resorted to using whatever she could muster to create her own infused version. Hita noticed she had not ventured out of the kitchen since their arrival and popped in see how she was. "They know about you and Rob," Hita said, "I had to tell them something, otherwise we would have had to explain your absence when they arrived."

She felt awful about Hita being left to explain their situation, she already had enough to contend with and there was very little she was able to do to change things. She was in the early stages of a passionate relationship with a man she had only just met. Whilst she may have loved and deeply cared during her past relationships, she had to be brutally honest with herself she had never actually been in love with any one before Rob. She anticipated the spark between them would only intensify, but Rob was married and although he and his ex-wife had been separated for some time they had not divorced. There would be a lot for them to discuss going forward. Would she be able to cope with it all? Would Rob feel the same way about her once she returned to the UK? Only time would tell.

With the kitchen returned to its former state and the meal almost ready. She joined Rob who was seated on the veranda with Spud and Paul. To her dismay she caught the tail-end of a deep discussion Paul was having with Rob. Paul was questioning Rob about his intentions towards her. She remembered Hita confiding to her about Paul having experienced a similar situation to hers, in the past with his ex-wife. As she sat next to Rob Paul asked him "So what happens now?" Rob reassuringly placed his hand on her knee and replied "Well, we will have to wait and see. What I do know is that I just had to see her before she left Australia." "We've got a lot of talking and figuring out to do, and at the moment I don't have all the answers." Paul replied "You took a risk, coming out here like this, does anyone else know?" Rob confirmed no else knew. Paul shook his head disapprovingly. "So what did you tell the Boss?" "I told him I needed the day off for a personal emergency" Rob stated. Spud sat silently throughout the discussion but looked uncomfortable. To change the subject she suggested that tea was ready and asked Paul to give her a hand to serve. After dinner she cleared the plates and tidied up the kitchen, they stayed behind for a beer before leaving. With the limited amount of time they had left together before she left Australia, they spent the rest of the time laughing, crying and making plans together for the future.

The cottage they had stayed in was located just a few minutes away from Paul and Hita's place. The morning had come where they would have to go their separate ways, it was a solemn occasion for them, but they were careful not to ruin the final moments they had together. They arranged to see each other again seven months later, although the seven months would be difficult, they were desperate to see each other again. Rob would start the divorce process with her back in the UK and she would return to the UK and arrange for Grimm to move out. She would also update Tia about Hita's invitation and her plans to return to Australia for a year; and to avoid causing Grimm any upset she would keep her new relationship strictly private.

The night before her departure she hardly slept, she had volunteered to sleep in the make-shift camp bed on her last night, due to an early departure early the following morning. Her departure had coincided with Paul's daughter Chloe's twelfth birthday party. With Paul's entire family staying over to celebrate. She wasn't happy about leaving but she was keen to make a start on her new plans for the future. She would miss them all, however with plans firmly in place for her return to Australia her flight back could not have occurred at a more convenient moment, she needed to get back so she could sort her life out before her return. Hita worried they would not make it to the airport in time and did her best to top up Ashton's breastfeeds as much as possible before leaving for the airport. Paul put her luggage in the boot of the Hita's vehicle; there was a large farewell party to see her off before she left. She individually said her farewells, and looked forward to seeing them again the following year. Spud gave her a comforting hug and a kiss; he appeared saddened at her departure and asked her what she planned to do regarding Rob, she kept her response brief and stated she could not say for definite, until she visited the next year. Hita and Paul had plans to visit the UK later that year and would be taking Spud and Pat with them and they promised to meet up when they got there.

With Ashton safely strapped inside the vehicle, Hita fastened her seat belt and started the car. They had not had time to eat breakfast with the others and Paul had been kind enough to prepare sandwiches for them to eat on the way. Whilst saying goodbye to Paul she became quite emotional and instructed Paul to take good care of Hita and the boys, he eagerly reassured her he would and worried that she was becoming too upset. She had not anticipated how sad she would have been at the prospect of leaving them. Hita repeatedly tried to get her to cheer up, she worried she would be too upset to drive and wanted to avoid the risk of an accident on the way to the airport. She did her best to console herself, but she felt unable to contain her sadness. She apologised to Hita for not having been a better friend during recent years and worried she may have let her down in some way, by not being able to visit before.   Hita understood and confirmed nothing had changed for her in terms of their friendship.   She reminded Hita that she had attempted to visit twice before, however her previous attempts had failed to materialise.

Hita was upset with the suggestion and reassured her she had not been a bad friend or could ever let her down.   She felt relieved to hear that from Hita and remarked that her presence now turned out to be the right time for her.   All in all her life was about to completely transform, visiting Australia had been the best decision she had made that year and her life had already improved since her arrival she had a renewed focus and had never been more excited about the future. Hita asked if she felt Rob was a suitable candidate for her next relationship. She reassured her that even though it had only been a short time that they had to gotten to get to know each other.   She felt they had discovered something quite special between them and she was keen to explore that part of her future.

***

As they pulled into Melbourne International Airport, they both felt weary from all the crying they had done on the way there.   She convinced Hita not to remain at the airport to see her off; she did not want to run the risk of Ashton waking up which would only complicate matters for her return journey, besides she had a long journey home and all the family were eagerly awaiting her return. Together they removed her suitcase from the boot of the vehicle and said their final goodbyes. She urged Hita to begin making her way back home, and confirmed she would be in contact as soon as she arrived back in the UK.

Seated in the departure lounge waiting for her return flight after her luggage had been checked in, one of the airport stewards approached her with a survey to complete, regarding the facilities within the airport and her experience overall whilst in Australia. Her feedback was most complimentary, she had nothing negative to report during her time in Australia had been well spent and she considered it a complete success. The airport attendant had been most impressed with her glowing responses and stated she was glad she had picked her for the study. Immediately after Rob phoned, he was really saddened at her leaving. She reassured him she would be back as promised and confirmed how much she loved him. Rob called again just prior to her boarding and promised to remain in close contact until they saw each other again.

The return flight from Australia allowed her a moment of clarity to process how drastic her life was about to change. Not only did she have a possible future to plan abroad, but there was also a lot to sort out, prior to her leaving. She still had the task of informing Tia of her new plans and that would be hard. She thought about the best choice of vernacular to use when presenting the news, overall she did not want Tia to be too upset, it would involve a big change for the both of them. With the rest of the time she had on board she slept for the majority of it. Australia was eleven hours ahead of the UK and she would need to adjust to the times accordingly. She would need to get used to being awake when the majority of the UK would be asleep, just to maintain contact with Hita and Rob once back home. Twenty-five hours later in to the journey she heard the Pilot announce their arrival in to London Heathrow, whilst she may not have been particularly overjoyed to be back in the country she was eager to get started on preparing for her new life abroad.

She made her way in to the customs area and felt instantly fed up with the hordes of passengers already waiting in line to be processed through immigration before exiting the airport. The customs area reminded her of a chaotic cattle market. She estimated there were least a hundred people waiting in the line ahead of her. She found an airport attendant who was busy assisting another passenger and waited impatiently for him to finish. She was keen to ascertain whether there was a quicker process of escaping the ever lengthening queue. The attendant informed her that the quickest way out of the airport unfortunately was to join the main queue. The attendant added due to the numbers of passengers currently in line they had laid on extra staff to assist with immigration and the queue was now moving quite rapidly. The attendant had been correct in his estimation, within twenty minutes of waiting in line she had managed to scan her passport through the barriers and waited to be summoned by a customs officer. As she approached the pod where the female officer was seated, she denoted an air of nonchalance. Instead of requesting to see her passport, the officer outstretched her hand out and gestured for it, prior to permitting her clearance. With luggage in tow she made her way towards the arrivals area. Her phoned vibrated and displayed part of a text message Grimm had sent. He was at Heathrow Airport and waiting for her in Arrivals.

She felt in no particular rush to meet with Grimm and popped in to the ladies toilet to freshen up. She had not yet decided how she would broach the news to him regarding her future plans, until then she would play it by ear. She had not seen Grimm until he approached her. It was an awkward encounter between them, they exchanged pleasantries and he enquired about the return journey. He asked whether she was hungry, she agreed she was a little peckish and they popped in to Café Rouge restaurant based within the Terminal. They talked briefly about her holiday and she expressed how much she had enjoyed her time there and was glad she had made the effort to go. Grimm told her he had missed her and she returned the compliment, deep down she had not felt that way and had been glad of the time they had apart. She did not have it within her to hurt him unnecessarily and wondered about his reasons for missing her when they were no longer a couple. She asked about Tia and how she had managed without her, she had missed her dearly and had no doubts she felt the same. She wondered how Tia would cope with her in Australia, Tia was twenty-three years old and considered a grown woman, she had to accept that Tia no longer needed her Mum dictating her life, on the contrary Tia would be best served living her own life with the added reassurance Mum was just a phone call away if needed.

As they left the airport to start the long journey home, she began to reminisce about her time spent away. She talked about the camping trip much to Grimm's amusement, all the while ensuring she kept her new relationship out of the conversation. By the time they had returned home, Grimm had been updated about her plans to return to Australia and he seemed genuinely happy for her. It was still quite early when they arrived home and Tia was not due back until later that afternoon. She quickly sent her a text, confirming she was back and looked forward to seeing her after work. As she headed towards her bedroom her mobile began vibrating. She was ecstatic to hear Rob on the other end, she had worried she may not hear from him again with her being out of the country. Rob was oblivious to her insecurities. She closed the bedroom door behind her and they spoke at length, even though they were ten and half thousand miles apart, the spark they had between them was ever present.

She had made the decision initially not to inform Tia about her relationship with Rob; Tia has endured enough recently, following her separation with Grimm, until she felt the time was right to do so, her main concern was to spend as much time as she could with her daughter as possible prior to her leaving. Later that evening following another phone conversation with Rob, she had received a text message from Grimm wondering about the status of their relationship, she was a little taken aback by the nature of his suggestion. Their decision to part as a couple had transpired completely due to Grimm's poor decisions that ultimately ended things between them. Once she had become aware of his constant flirting at work and his decision to move in with a female colleague and not bothering to inform her about it, until two months later. Grimm had let her down in the best way possible, and had shown no regards whatsoever for her feelings. In retrospect she found it difficult to comprehend why he seemed to now have a change of heart.

For her it was four years too late to try and salvage their relationship, she was with Rob now and she believed this was the real thing. She could not recall a time when she had felt this strongly about someone. She replied to Grimm's text and mentioned her time in Australia had not changed her decision about them. She also informed him that whilst she preferred things to remain amicable, she expressed the need for him to move out of the family home. Grimm confirmed he would be moving out the following day and would return to Peterborough to continue living with Mena. She was saddened he was moving so far away, but accepted his decision.

Tia was still baffled by her recent admission and enquired whether she was sure about her decision to go to Australia. She reassured her she could not wait to begin her life over and that she had no intentions of missing out on the once in a lifetime opportunity. She briefly mentioned her relationship with Rob, not wanting to make it sound more than it was, to her it was still early days between them and she wanted to be certain about where they were heading before she offered any further details. Tia was happy for her and felt she deserved to meet someone worthwhile. She had been disappointed with the way things had ended for her with Grimm, but having witnessed first-hand the birthday card episode, she no longer regarded him as a worthy contender for her Mother. Tia was deeply affected by her decision to leave the country; she had not foreseen a time her mum would no longer reside in the same country. She would have preferred her to stay, so she could assist in helping her grow her new business. She reminded Tia of the missed opportunities she had to stay at Hita's before and that if things had worked out accordingly back then, it was likely they would both been living in Australia now and informed her she was welcome to join her if she wanted. Her plans to leave the UK on paper appeared all figured out, however she knew as the time to leave drew near it would be almost impossible to leave her precious daughter behind.

***

Bali

They had been longing for this day ever since her return to the UK and it would be the centre of their discussions leading up to it. With only ten days to go before they would be finally reunited, the past seven and a half months they had patiently waited had certainly taken its toll on the both of them. She began to stress to the point of going doolally and it was becoming increasingly apparent to those that knew her well. At work she felt highly strung, lacked patience with her colleagues and was super over-sensitive. She had noticed her colleagues were becoming distant towards her to avoid being the target of her frustrations. The upcoming holiday should have been a period of excitement for her; instead it was turning in to one of self-doubt for both parties. They had made huge inroads together, being so far apart they had overcome many obstacles that had brought them closer together. However as the time neared for them to be reunited, Rob wondered whether she would still find him attractive as they had been so long apart. She did her best to convince him otherwise, in trying to do so she created her own insecurities and wondered whether Rob was less attracted to her, even though he had never mentioned it.

He admitted that whilst he believed there had been no change in their relationship and considered them very much a couple. He had been struggling with his decision about them long term and would not be able to make a permanent decision until they met in Bali. Rob had not been prepared for the negative affect his admission would have on her. They frequently bickered about the limbo of their relationship and at times they were unable to reach an agreement. The distance between them only added weight to Rob's foresight making it all the more unsettling for her. She couldn't understand why he was unable to make a decision before Bali; her main concern meant that he may have a change of heart and she would find it difficult to accept should he change his mind.

She arrived at Denpasar Airport at almost midnight arriving in to a country she had never been to where she knew no one, except Rob and they had only been together a few months. She felt quite nervous. Instead of following the other passengers to the immigration queues at customs, she entered the ladies bathroom to freshen up. Her Prince Charming was somewhere on the other side of the airport and the only thing that stood between them was the internal barriers. She wondered if Rob was as anxious to see her as she was to see him after so long. She wanted to make sure the first time he saw her, he would be happy he had made the trip. Her hair had begun to stick to her forehead due to the intensity of the humidity, she quickly sorted it refreshed her make-up and dabbed on her favourite perfume Chloè and walked over to the immigration area.

There were only a few remaining passengers waiting to be processed, she asked a security attendant which queue she needed to join, after confirming she was traveling on a British passport she was advised she could attend any of the queues she desired. After being processed by immigration she made her way nervously through the duty free area, as she did so she quickly glanced at the imposing crowd directly facing her. They consisted of mainly of Balinese Taxi drivers, frantically waving their welcome plaques and those without, pleaded with her to use their mini-cab services. The scenes she observed reminded her of absolute chaos and disorder. Some of the offenders were being quite persistent and followed her direction until she was out of view; she prayed that Rob would appear very soon and rescue her from the madness. She checked with one of the duty-free staff whether she was heading in the right direction to exit the airport. Having cleared the arrivals area she proceeded to walk towards the right-hand side of the airport, uncertain of where she should position herself. In the near distance she noticed Rob standing nervously just a few feet away from her, wearing her favourite green and white singlet. Rob looked slightly flushed in the face and kept his hands firmly in his pocket smiling as she approached him. As their eyes met she nervously returned his smile, hoping she didn't trip over her suitcase as she made her way over to where he was waiting.

As she approached him he opened his arms and welcomed her to Bali, they embraced holding each other closely for a while as they looked in to each other's eyes. She asked whether he was alright and he confirmed he was now that she had arrived. He whispered she looked amazing and felt the weight loss suited her. She was pleased with his response regarding her appearance, she had fasted and completed three daily powerwalks in order, to be as in-shape as she was. Rob confided due to the anticipation of waiting to see her after so long meant he urgently needed to visit the bathroom, as well as locating Alex his designated driver to take them to the hotel. Rob found Alex en route to the bathroom and briefly introduced them before rushing inside. Alex gave an official welcome to Bali using their customary greeting, he joined his hands together as if in prayer and bowed, unaware of how she should respond, she mimicked his actions and extended her gratitude.

They engaged in small talk regarding the sultry temperatures and she apologised for the lateness of her arrival. Alex appeared quite down to earth and although pint-sized in stature his protruding muscles were undeniable. Alex had a similar character to Rob she found him quite sociable, personable and humorous. Rob reappeared after a few minutes and they headed to the car park. Alex and his assistant met up with them a few minutes later having retrieved their vehicle. She felt guilty as they struggled to load her heavy suitcase in to the back of the boot and she thanked them all extensively for collecting her from the Airport. Rob stated he did not mind waiting; he had been to visit Alex and his family at their home, before coming to meet her.

The journey to the hotel took almost forty-five minutes, it was now the early hours of the morning, but it appeared as if the area they were driving through had just started to liven up. The area outside of the airport was very busy, there were lots of people milling about and the traffic was congested in all directions. The environment reminded her of a party like atmosphere; those that were hanging around appeared in no hurry and there was an array of bright colours accompanied by palm trees and ornate architecture that encompassed its surroundings. She had never seen anything like it before and was pleased she had managed to talk Rob into meeting her there. She had snuggled in the back seat of the vehicle with Rob and found she couldn't contain herself and could not believe they were actually together after such a long time and kept him close to her during the car ride. Rob appeared to enjoy the attention she lavished upon him and returned the affection she showed him by kissing her fondly. Alex parked the car at the entrance of the hotel; Rob removed her suitcase from the boot and informed Alex and his driver that they would be able to manage the rest of the way. She followed Rob as he led the way to their villa, he told her that the accommodation was fairly old fashioned; but was fully air-conditioned and comfortable enough for them. She was pleased with the location of the villa, it was situated in the rear of the complex and from the outside it appeared quite spacious. After heading inside Rob ran a shower for her, she was just about to step inside when he opted to join her. She noticed they were still so comfortable in the presence of each other, despite the long absence, it was as if they had never been apart and it helped to reaffirm that Rob was the right companion for her. They dried themselves off after showering and got in to bed; although they were suffering with sleep deprivation they shared a moment of intimacy for the first time since they had seen each other, before falling asleep.

Early the next morning and keen to get the first official day of their holiday underway, Rob suggested they went for an early morning stroll. She wore a mini blue, white and black striped mesh designer dress with flip flops, Rob passed his approval on her choice of outfit before they headed to the beach. It was still quite muggy from the night before and the sun had put in an early appearance. The Garden View Resort hotel they were staying in was small and intimate, unlike other hotels she had frequented. The hotel was in the middle stages of renovation work, the extension being erected did nothing to detract their time together. Rob had befriended a few of the builders on site, and they would converse whenever they used the swimming pool. Having returned from their stroll Rob showed her how to use the facilities inside the villa. He directed her to where the safe was positioned and informed her of the code, she thought it was a good time to hand him his early birthday present as she would not be able to join in with the celebrations on the day itself, Rob unwrapped the silver-linked chain she had bought for him and she handed him a few designer t-shirts she had purchased, finally she presented him with eighteen million Indonesian Rupiah the equivalent of a thousand pounds to be used as spending money between them.

Rob was completely blown away by the gesture; he was stunned with the effort she had made for him, including her generosity. She reminded him of the few doubters he had told her about that had been negative about their relationship when they heard of their holiday plans. Some had suggested she was only interested in using him for his money and when his ex-wife found out about their plans she had the gall to suggest Rob had paid for the entire trip. The money she had given him was considered equivalent to that of a millionaire in Bali, and an indication that her feelings towards him were nothing other than genuine; even so she would never have considered travelling on holiday without making a valid contribution her end. Rob was stunned by her explanation and reluctantly accepted the funds. She had over exceeded his expectations he told her he had never met anyone before her who thought who had made the efforts that she had.

After visiting much of the area near to the complex where they stayed, they headed for a swim back at the hotel. The intensity from the heat of the sun had them eager to cool off. Rob selected the white Ted Baker bikini from the collection of designer swimwear she had taken with her. She took a dip in the pool and sat on one of the built-in stools situated in the corner of the pool bar. Rob completed a breast stroke covering the full length of the pool and then swam back towards her. They drank a couple of Bintang beers and held each other as they floated in the pool and mingled with the other hotel guests.

Carmel and her husband Jack were also patrons at the same hotel and soon introduced themselves to the couple. Carmel stated she felt drawn to get to know them better; she had observed the interaction between them and described their affection for one another as infectious. She complimented them on their relationship and remarked she was able to tell when a couple genuinely cared about each other. She stated they were meant to be and felt they were well suited together. Rob confirmed they had been a couple only seven months and that it was the second time they had been able to see each other since the start of their long-distance relationship. Carmel was intrigued by what he told her and enquired how they managed to make it work between them. Rob stated the relationship had not been without its share of sacrifice and difficulties and that their story was a complicated one that was better saved for a later discussion on another occasion. Carmel identified with the challenges Rob had mentioned and disclosed she had been married to Jack for over thirty years and that they had faced problems within their marriage, they had been able to overcome, Carmel wished them well and looked forward to catching up with them again during their stay.

***

The Garden View Resort was a cottage-style establishment, the majority of the staff employed were extremely hospitable and friendly especially the bar staff Mundey and Kendu, who were quite popular amongst the other patrons. Rob had been to Bali on at least four occasions compared to Carmel and Jack who had been to Bali forty–eight times and would stay at the location sometimes up to three times per year. During their stay they met another couple

Vivian and Michael Conroy who were also from Victoria, Melbourne and a few days later they were befriended by Monty, she was in her early twenties, and had been staying at the resort a few doors down from theirs with her parents. They had been to Bali on at least eight occasions and had made long terms friends with some of the Balinese natives who lived there.

Monty had observed her a few days before, walking through the hotel grounds unaccompanied and recalled at the time she felt she was a very attractive lady, and wondered who she might be staying with at the resort. Monty and her family were originally from New South Wales, but she was keen to move to Melbourne and felt the diversity and cosmopolitan lifestyle there better suited her personality. A week in to their holiday they met an older gentleman also staying at their hotel, although they had not exchanged any formal introductions, he was often seated pool side with a cigar in hand accompanied with a large goblet of beer and always made a point of acknowledging them whenever they were present. During their stay Rob bumped in to a friend Glen who was from Glengarry, he was staying in hotel nearby and they would see him often whenever they were out and about.

Wednesday 31st August 2016 was the day Rob had been looking forward to most during his stay. It was the day of the Australian Rugby semi-finals and he had arranged for a few of his friends that had flown in that day to watch it with them. Daz, Danny, Gail and Glen, Steve and Brittany, Audrey and Dave she had never met before. Rob was dressed in his teams colours black and white, she had chosen to wear what was fast becoming a favourite of Rob's a black tailored mini skirt with a crisp white off-the-shoulder gypsy blouse he had not seen her in before, accessorised with gladiator-style laced white patent sandals. Rob's friends had no idea she would be in attendance and he thought would be surprised to see them together. She worried his friends might not warm to her, without the advanced notice she would be in attendance. Rob had dated Gail's sister during their late teens, although things were very amicable between them, Rob had warned that Gail was not sure how she would take her being there. She had no idea what to make of it all but trusted Rob would see she came to no harm.

Rob's guests arrived as expected, they expressed their surprise of them being together, but made her welcome all the same dispelling any previous doubts or concerns she may have had. Gail and Audrey had made plans to go shopping and invited her to go with them, but she politely declined their kind offer, preferring to remain and watch the game. St. Kilda out skilled their opponents South Melbourne on the day and won the semi-finals, although they had not qualified for the finals themselves, Rob was ecstatic with the win and remained in good spirits throughout the day. She thought the St. Kilda Rugby Team had been mesmerising to watch, she was very impressed with their form and asked Rob to keep her updated on any future tournaments they played in. With the game now over, they said their farewells and arranged to meet up before leaving Bali. Rob also mentioned she would be joining him in Australia in a few months, Gail and her husband were pleased she would be returning to Australia and invited her to come over for a barbeque when she arrived. Gail and her Husband were scheduled to leave on the same return flight with Rob and promised to confirm the arrangements on the return journey.

A few days in to the trip following another hearty Balinese meal, they completed the usual routine of going to a place they had renamed 'Kissing Corner'. Rob had tenderly kissed her on the corner of Legian Street the first time they'd visited, the gesture remained etched in the minds of the locals who instantly recognised them whenever they frequented the area. As they approached the corner Rob became distracted by the commotion he heard behind him. She had also heard it and stopped to look behind her, the disturbance appeared to be coming from a group of people she did not recognise, but appeared acquainted to Rob. She had concerns about the group consisting of his ex-wife or daughters, and wondered if they had inappropriately tracked Rob down to the island to cause a scene.

Loryn and her daughters Trista and Melissa had made their contempt for her very clear. They had found out about their relationship six months after it had started. They regularly referred to her as either a 'black nigger' or a 'black bitch' whenever she was mentioned, however she had been spared the displeasure of meeting any of them yet. Rob had been appalled and hurt by their racist comments and confronted them about it. By choosing to defend their relationship he had simultaneously caused a major rift within the family and since then rarely heard from them. Rob was adamant he would not allow their interference to impact their relationship and believed he had a right to be happy.

She created some personal distance between Rob and the group, hoping to avoid being caught up in the melee. After a few minutes Rob motioned for her to join them and introduced her to the members of the group. Brian and Sue Lane, Lynn Shivers and Brooke Lynch-Delaney were all former colleagues of Rob's, Hita's and Paul's from the penal institution they once all worked at. They had remembered Rob would be in Bali during the time they would be there and had spent much of their holiday searching for him; with their mission completed the day they were due to leave. Brian and Sue had met and married whilst working at the jail, Lynn Shivers had worked closely with Rob, although her roots were Scottish she had only recently recovered from battling a long and debilitating illness and Brooke was a distant Cousin of Rob's through marriage.

The group had been in Bali for a month Sue and Brian were leaving that evening, Brooke and Lynn would return to join them a few days later. With the introductions completed with, they made their way over to their favourite bar 'Legends' and were greeted by the host Carlos Made who made them welcome, whilst they celebrated Brian and Sue's safe return. She found herself seated between Rob and Sue at the drinks table and was able to have a lengthy conversation with her. She mentioned Rob's upcoming trip to UK at the end of the year and told them about their plans to visit Rotterdam, Amsterdam and Leeuwarden whilst he was there. Sue and Brian also had plans to visit the UK at the same time Rob would be there and they made arrangements to meet up when they got there. She explained that during some of Rob's stay she would have to work though it would provide Rob some extra company whenever she would have to. Sue and Brian flights were due later that evening, but they still had packing to do, they said their farewells and arranged to meet with Lynn and Brooke before they were due to leave.

The day had arrived for Brooke and Lynn to leave Bali and so they popped in to see them before their flight. Their belongings were being loaded on to the van that would be taking them to the airport, they stopped in to Legends Bar for a final drink and both Lynn and Brooke offered to help her find employment when she arrived in Australia the following year. Lynn stated she had links to Australian government officials and would arrange a meeting with them when she arrived. Lynn was certain they'd have a few openings and would be able to assist her in finding employment and they would provide her with character references to support her applications. She had not been prepared for their kind offers of generosity and became emotional.

She had worried her opportunity to obtain a visa was slipping by because of her age. Her mini-breakdown soon reduced Brooke to tears, unhappy to be leaving the island before she was ready to. Lynn and Brook travelled to Bali yearly and invited them to join them there the following August. The invitation appealed to them Rob enjoyed travelling to Bali and had considered building a house there and believed a permanent home on the island was a viable option. Lynn and Brooke encouraged Rob to do so and stated it would be a worthwhile investment and if he chose to follow through with his plans they would be keen to rent the property when they visited. They finished their drinks and walked them back to their hotel; the mini-van had been loaded and ready to take them back to the airport. They wished then a safe flight and promised to keep in touch; Lynn gave her a straw hat before boarding the van and she returned the compliment and gifted Lynn a tiger-print dress she owned that had been a favourite of hers.

They spent the remainder of their holiday either sightseeing or visiting the Y-Sports bar, a venue attached to the resort they stayed in. Rob usually placed a bet on the horses whenever he visited, but had not won any of the bets he placed until a few days before they were due to leave, he was paid out one hundred and fifty Indonesian Rupiah, the only win he had during his time there. She asked him not to place any further bets, believing his luck had run out. Rob agreed with her and believed the betting steward was responsible for his run of bad luck.

Later they met with Anna, she was a close friend of Rob's and they had known each other since Rob had first travelled to Bali. Anna owned a beauty spa; Rob was a regular customer whenever he was in town. On the first day of their holiday Rob had mistakenly popped in to what he thought was Anna's spa, only to be informed a few days later, that the spa he had used belonged to someone else. Anna's business had expanded since they had last seen each other and her spa relocated nearer to the hotel they were staying in. During Rob's final visit to the shop Rob complained he had not been happy with the prices Anna had charged, the total bill had come to twenty-two thousand Indonesian Rupiah, Rob had offered Anna twenty thousand, but Anna insisted he paid the extra two thousand she had initially quoted. She thought Rob was being unreasonable, compared to the astronomical prices charged in the UK, Anna's fee of just twelve pounds fifty each for two feet massages and a hand massage was hard to compete with in her opinion. They would also treat themselves to an array of massages and holistic treatments from Bonito's spa with any free time they managed to squeeze.

Prior to being with Rob she had not been sexually active for the past four years, Rob was totally in tune with his own sexuality and had an insatiable appetite for it she had not experienced before. She felt her sensuality had been put on the back burner for far too long. Rob proved to be very experienced in these matters and they complimented each other sensually during their mammoth sexual encounters. Following another session of passion between them, Rob on this occasion seemed somewhat different and had been perspiring profusely as well as breathless. Although he seemed content she became concerned after little perspiration droplets rolled off his forehead and in to her hair. Thereafter Rob was noticeably still breathing heavily, looking as flushed as ever he made his way to the shower in complete silence.

She wondered if she had done something wrong or had upset him in some way without being aware of it. She followed him in to the bathroom and checked he was okay, he stated he was but didn't appear to be. She checked with him again because she was had her own doubts. Rob reiterated he was okay and told her not to worry. Rob left the bathroom after his shower still barely speaking to her; unconvinced she also took a shower and could hear him speaking on the phone whilst seated on the hotel veranda. She assumed he was speaking with Treen, who had always been supportive of their relationship and someone they both trusted.

With her shower finished she heard Rob tap the apartment window from the outside vying for her attention. She went outside to join him and spoke briefly with Treen. When the call ended, she spoke to Rob and said she was concerned since their moment together he had become so distant and quiet and it was making her question his feelings towards her. Rob apologised stating that was the best love making they had ever had and in his opinion it had increased his feelings towards her and whilst he may have felt slightly breathless he had no other concerns. He assured her she ticked all the right boxes for him. After hearing his explanation she simply leaned over and kissed him passionately expelling her relief.

With only two days remaining until the end of their holiday, Rob seemed especially down. Neither of them were looking forward to being parted again, after making the long journey back to their respective domains. For the second time in their relationship they would to be would be apart for three and a half months until they would see each other again, when Rob would travel to England to see her. They enjoyed a leisurely morning stroll to the beach and then decided to head off to The Garuder, hoping to meet up with another of Rob's ex-colleagues Danny from the penal institution.

Danny owned a leather store in Legian, Lynn had mentioned they visit the store to get some leather items made; whilst they spent time with Danny before they left. She was a shoe freak prior to leaving Bali she had purchased twenty-eight pairs of shoes, in addition to the pairs Danny had made for her during her stay. They were having trouble locating Danny and the store he owned, a local taxi driver tried to assist them, however due to the language barrier, the assistance he was able to offer was limited. Still without luck she suggested they went for breakfast and would contact Danny by phone. Danny confirmed he would be out for most of the day and would no plans to return until late that afternoon. With their plans scuppered they made their way back to Legian. Rob called in to visit a tattooist he knew along the way, the tattoo parlour had relocated, however the bar staff next door did not have the new address the parlour had since moved to.

On the way back to their hotel Rob called in to 'Apache Tattoo' studio, the studio was owned and managed by Angie Dow an Australian lady from Queensland, who had moved to the island for four years ago. Angie had not heard of the tattoo parlour Rob had been looking for, after making a few enquiries with her regarding the possibility of getting a design completed, Angie quickly organised a tattooist to begin the procedure. Rob surprised her with a replica of a tattoo she had designed six months earlier incorporating his initials. She was blown away with Rob's decision to get an identical design with her initials and thought it was a fitting tribute to her. Whilst she waited for Rob's tattoo to get underway, she mentioned to Angie that she had been missing her Dad and was considering getting a tattoo done to honour him. She showed Angie a photo of the design Vivian had done the day before, to commemorate a dear friend who had passed away recently. Angie checked online and found a similar motif that had the word 'Dad' etched in to it. She liked the simplicity of the design and asked Rob what he thought. Rob was completely against the idea at first, however slowly came around to her way of thinking knowing how much it meant to her.

With his new tattoo completed, Rob enquired about the possibility of recolouring the Disney characters on his upper torso that were at least twenty years old. The work would be extensive and would take at least four hours to complete. Keen to get the work started Angie arranged for the recolouring to be completed there and then, her design would be started after Rob's recolouring to avoid having to change the needles in between. Following a short cigarette break Ableh was ready to begin the recolouring work, with the needle poised and ready to go the shop fell in complete darkness. Angie suspected they had suffered a power cut, due to renovation works nearby. Until the power was restored they would be unable to complete any further work. Angie arranged for Ableh and his assistant Bob to use her mopeds and ferry them back to their hotel, she would also arrange for them to be collected once the power was reinstated. Lounging poolside whilst they waited, she could hear Luther Vandross's classic 'Dance with my Father' playing in the background. She became emotional the song was pulling on her emotions and made her visibly upset, Rob held her as she tried to compose herself, as the song ended they received a text from Angie stating the power had been restored and Ableh and Bob were on their way to the hotel to collect them.

With the tattoos completed they returned to the beach to visit a friend of Rob's, Harry who he had met on a previous visit. Harry was a keen fisherman and owned a small business selling beverages on the beach, Rob conducted the introductions and they toasted on a few Bintang's as they watched the other tourists and rated the best bikini bodies. They also visited Bonito's Spa for a final couples massage and stopped in at Poser's Bar for a light lunch. She chose the calamari and chips with garlic and herb mayonnaise dip and Rob opted for the Chicken Sauté skewers with fried rice. They enjoyed a last swim and indulged in a couple of drinks with Jack and Carmel's husband. For dinner she had chosen a little black dress she had first purchased with Rob in mind. They were going to be dining at Uncle Norm's a formal restaurant that Lynn had highly recommended.

Rob was impressed with her choice of attire and judging by the admiring looks and shouts of "You're a very lucky man" from many of the locals they passed; Rob appeared to be in awe of the admiring glances and comments being directed at them and told her felt like the luckiest man on the island. On the way to dinner they stopped at Fat Bowl Keung Restaurant, they had dined there before but popped in for pre-dinner drinks and people-watched whilst they reminisced over the times they had shared, careful to avoid the topic of her early flight the next day. After dinner they popped in to Billy's for a final farewell drink, Jack called in for a couple and they all left together and stopped in at Uncle Norm's a bistro restaurant, Jack had been suggested keen to see the live band playing that evening.

Jack remained at the bar area whilst they opted to dine inside having built up an appetite, due to the earlier drinking and settled for the fried rice. Whilst eating they became aware of a large group of rowdy teenagers seated on the table next to them. None of the girls were wearing bras and the low-cut tops they wore were barely covering their modesty and their ample bosoms were very much becoming the focus of the entire restaurant, due to their drunken antics to the delight of the male waiters who were struggling to keep up with their demands.   The three of them left and made their way back to Billy's for the second time that evening, as they approached the main entrance Rob's pace began to quicken and without any warning he grabbed her by the hand and dragged her in to the middle of the dance floor.

The venue was packed and the live band had just begun their performance, Rob pulled her in close and they slow danced to the band's rendition of Ronan Keating's 'When you say nothing at all'. The majority of the other patrons cooed alongside with them, as they took centre stage. As the song neared its end one of the male hosts who Rob knew well, came up to her from behind and with a feather duster he ran it up and down the back of her legs. This was the second time the host had played this prank on her, to the amusement of the audience who enjoyed the comedy of it all.

They were seated at the front bar of Billy's enjoying a beer when the group of braless girls last seen at Uncle Norms entered the bar to the pleasure of the male hosts. A short while after, a girl from the group walked over to where they were seated and introduced herself to them. Beth was from Perth and was keen to tell them about her plans to relocate to Melbourne once she returned from her holiday. Beth and her friends had travelled to Bali for her eighteenth birthday with her parents' consent. Jack was concerned for her welfare and discussed the possible pitfalls of being in Bali, drunk and provocatively dressed and forewarned if she were to incur any problems whilst on the island, she could contact him as a point of reference.   Jack was well acquainted with the Chief Prosecutor and a few of the Government officials on the island.

It was approaching midnight and she still needed to pack before her flight the next morning, before leaving the venue, Jack dared Rob to approach the drag queens hosts located outside the bar opposite, Jack was particularly keen for Rob to approach the one sporting a blonde afro. Not one to back down on a dare, they crossed the street and headed towards the gay bar. There were now two drag queens standing outside attempting to drum more custom. Rob approached the lady boys from behind and grabbed them by the waist, she meanwhile made her way to the front of where they were standing, desperately trying to keep a straight face as she photographed them together. Jack was still inside Billy's observing Rob in action and while struggling to maintain his composure he almost fell off his bar stool. She could not hold it together any longer and her eyes began to water as she burst in to fits of laughter. With the prank over Jack joined them and they all walked back to the hotel, reminiscing about their antics on the way. Rob and Jack stopped off in the Y-Sports Bar for a quick beer they were insistent she tagged along with them, but with time running out before she was due to leave, she politely declined the offer and left them to it and returned to the villa to pack her belongings.

With her suitcase packed she had some time on her hands, Rob had not yet returned from the Sports Bar so she began to pack his luggage. Rob's flight was also due the next day but he was scheduled on a late evening flight. With the packing completed she contemplated the difficulties she would face not being able to see Rob for the next three and a half months. She was pleased they had made the impromptu decision to see each other for the New Year, otherwise they would have had to wait another seven and a half months, when she was due to return to Australia. She was not looking forward to waking up at two in the morning ahead of check-in. Her flight was not due to leave until ten past seven, but she was required to be at the airport four hours before her flight. Alex had sent one of his drivers to take them to the airport; after arriving at the airport the driver kindly offered to wait for an hour, allowing them some time to themselves before leaving to go their separate ways.

Inside the airport they ventured into a small diner and ordered tea and toast; attempting to lighten the sombre mood Rob told her he had not wanted their time together to end. As she listened to Rob speaking about how much he had enjoyed their time together, she became emotional; she shared the same sentiments as he did about the holiday. Rob eyes were now watering and she was worried about leaving him on his own. She was more in love with him than she had ever been and could not wait for him to visit her in the UK. Rob had been even more receptive to the idea now that she was leaving, than when she had initially mentioned it. It had been one of the first topics he had mentioned when they first saw each other in Bali. Rob's willingness to reconsider visiting the UK had been such an unexpected surprise for her and in complete contrast to how he had felt previously. In the past they had bickered over the idea, she had felt he had shown a lack of interest in visiting her there; whereby Rob had wanted to ensure the magic between them still existed when they met in Bali before further committing himself to the idea.

With the end of the hour almost in sight they both had tears in their eyes, she had just about managed to compose herself and desperately wished they had more time together. Deep down they were under no illusions, it didn't matter how long they were able to spend together; leaving to go their separate ways would be extremely difficult under the circumstances. Rob told her how much he would miss her and with the time he had until his flight, after she departed would be difficult for him to remain there without her company. He told her she was perfect for him and held all the qualities he was looking for in a companion. She had longed to hear his sentiments about her, he thanked her for looking after him during their stay and she reciprocated to him that she felt the same about him and was happy he was looking forward to his trip in December, so they could spend the New Year together. The year two thousand and seventeen would turn out to be the permanent start of their life together, when she would be joining him within five weeks of his return to Australia.

Whilst seated in the breakfast diner Rob became frustrated with the lack of service being offered by the waiting staff and began stating his objections. Attempting to diffuse the situation from escalating, she approached the waiting staff and asked for the accompaniments for the teas they had ordered, she also enquired about the time the toast would take to arrive, noting it had taken well over ten minutes to receive any of the items they had requested. After breakfast she persuaded Rob to leave the airport she feared the cab driver would not be willing to wait any longer and did not want him to incur any complications in returning to the hotel.

As Rob began to leave the airport it suddenly dawned on her how alone she felt without him, as she walked over to the check-in area flashbacks of some of their poignant moments began to encapsulate her mind. She wondered what Rob was up to at that moment, was he feeling the same way about her; was he coping without her being there. The flight from Bali to Brunei did not going accordingly, which she felt was unusual for this airline, soon after being seated on the tiny aircraft, the air hostess managed to let a couple of pillows fall onto her head twice from the overhead compartment twice. She believed the air stewardess had been oblivious of her indiscretion at the time, due to the lack of apology received. The breakfast meal offered on board the flight consisted of three soya chicken pieces, rice and courgettes in a sweet Piccalilli sauce all of which she loathed. She was glad she had stuck with her decision to opt for the Oriental Vegetarian meal as opposed to the alternative, having witnessed another passenger seated opposite discard the Chicken Sausage meal, after the first bite.

It was three minutes to ten in the morning when she arrived in Brunei; the connecting flight to Dubai was not scheduled until five to eight in the evening, with only a few Brunei Dollars remaining, she requested a large cup of hot water from the airport cafeteria. During the flight she had suffered a severe bout of diarrhoea on the flight earlier, which she quickly put down to the Lobster she had indulged in the night before. Trying to fill the time she had until her flight was due she made enquiries with the Bureau De Change about converting some currency and was poorly advised by the

Teller to complete any exchanges once she returned to the UK, in order to avoid having to convert the currency twice. Had she completed the transaction in Brunei the currency would have to be converted into Bruneian Dollars before it was transferred in to Sterling, prior to receiving any dividends.

The Teller advised the process would be more cost-effective and she would receive more for her money due to being converted just once. She had not been prepared for the nine hour wait between connecting flights and had trouble comprehending that the only plane to Dubai from Brunei was the one she had been scheduled on to take. To fill in the time she began people-watching until she finally dosed off for a couple of hours. When she awoke she was horrified to find she was the only person remaining in that part of the airport, the other passengers from her flight were nowhere in sight and for a moment she thought she might be the only passenger travelling back to the UK. She became momentarily distracted with a group of young teenaged boys she assumed were waiting for their connecting flight, she watched them as they toured the confined airport and played catch with a tennis ball.

At approximately four-thirty she was approached by another traveller Nancy who had travelled to Brunei from the Philippines. Nancy had a friendly disposition and had immediately taken a shine to her. Nancy enquired whether Gate One was the correct gate for boarding the Manilla flight that was scheduled to depart at seven that evening, she confirmed it was and informed her of her own dilemma having arrived at the airport that morning and so far there had been no listings displayed or information provided for her flight that was expected to depart later that evening. She found it difficult to fathom that her plane was due to leave just fifty-five minutes after Nancy's and could not understand why Nancy's flight was being displayed more than three hours prior to its departure.

Nancy instantly dispelled her concerns and reassured her that she had faith her flight would be displayed on the board soon. They continued talking until her flight details were finally showing an hour and a half later. Nancy explained her reason for travelling was as a result of an emergency within her family. Nancy's sister was expected to pass away any day due to being terminally ill with cancer; her Mum had not wanted her to make the journey and disagreed with her decision to visit them. Nancy's Mother believed there was nothing she could do to improve her sister's condition and informed her she would not even be able to touch her sister when she visited the hospital. Nancy felt strongly about being present for her family and believed that it was important she put in an appearance rather than working just to earn money back in the Philippines. She agreed with Nancy wholeheartedly about her reasons for making the trip, especially having heard about her sister's Husband who was also undergoing life changing surgery to have both legs amputated, due to an ongoing battle with Diabetes. Her sister and brother in-law also had a young daughter they were struggling to take care of due to their illnesses, with Nancy's flight scheduled for boarding she wished her a safe journey and her family well.

The flight from Brunei to Dubai was pretty much as disappointing as the earlier flight to Brunei had been; there was a young baby seated in the first row of the left aisle that screamed the entire flight; she had been seated in the right aisle without the extra leg room that had been promised earlier by the Balinese Flight Attendant she had checked-in with. The aisle seat she had been allocated was next to a young Muslim lady who was dressed in the oldest pair of beige socks with the soles completely covered in black flint, she felt the condition of the socks were offensive, yet the owner of the owner of them had no qualms in crossing her legs in a Lotus position, whereby her feet rested in the adjoining seats.

Although they were on a large plane with plenty of room, the offensive passenger was treating the premium economy seat as if she was sat at home impervious of the other passengers seated either side of her and held her posture the entire flight. On at least three occasions she found herself speaking sternly to the female passenger about removing her offensive paws completely away from her seat and blanket. To add to her discomfort there was a female passenger seated in the row directly behind her, absurdly she been assigned a window seat and spent much of the flight either wrenching or vomiting from the very pit of her stomach repeatedly most of the flight, very much to the upset of the other travellers also seated in that section.

She felt nauseous every time the passenger had a motion and prayed that both female travellers would be travelling no further than Dubai once they arrived. To avoid the temptation of continuously moaning about the passengers who were making her journey unbearable, she plugged in her personal headphones and set them on loud to assist in drowning out the offending behaviours in attempt to find peace of mind, only to be awoken and informed a few hours later by one of the flight attendants, they had been trying to rouse her during the flight for something to eat and drink, unfortunately the steward was regretful not to be able to offer her the vegetarian option she had pre-ordered, that had been given to another passenger. Although disappointed she accepted the disappointment gracefully and accepted the replacement beef dish that had been offered. All in all her journey took a total of thirty hours across four different countries, she had not been able to compute the extensive travelling she had completed until she returned home, she was proud of her achievements and the memories she had made, her legs and feet had swollen beyond belief, but as painful as they were she accepted it as part of the course.

***

Since her return from Bali she had been working flat out to prepare for Rob's arrival to the UK. She no longer slept in at the weekends and with whatever spare time she had available, she used wisely to deep clean the entire house and began the painstaking task of clearing any unwanted furniture and personal items she would not be able to take with her to Australia. Upon their arrivals to their respective homes they soon picked up where they had left off, hoping to dispel the lull that followed after their time spent together. They only had a three and half month wait prior to being reunited once more. Rob struggled the most during their time apart and often complained how difficult he was finding life without her. She shared Rob's sentiments but needed this time to focus on organising the house for his impending stay as well as her own departure a few weeks thereafter, with the added task of saving enough finance ahead of their trip to Amsterdam where Rob was planning on visiting the birth places of his late Dutch parents. Time was very much of the essence for her with Rob in the UK she would be unable to organise much her own departure during his three week stay, giving her just five weeks to organise herself before she was able to join them in Australia and she had grave concerns whether she would be able to accomplish it all.

At times she felt overly stretched trying to achieve all the outstanding tasks concerning her move. It was not until Rob's feelings regarding her absence were so heightened during a phone call; Rob had mentioned to her had he anticipated beforehand how difficult it was going to be coping without her, it was likely he would have contemplated ending their relationship. On hearing his remarks she felt overwhelmed and informed him he was being selfish and inconsiderate of her feelings with the stress of it all. She reminded him of the sacrifices she had made attempting to get everything done in time for his arrival and wondered how she was going to cope when it came to leaving her daughter and family behind to join him and yet he had the gall to contemplate backing out on their arrangements.

Rob reassured her he had no desire to act upon his negative thoughts and continued to complain about how much he missed her and blamed his outburst on the great times they had spent together. He began to cry and stated he wished she was coming to Australia even earlier than they had planned. She understood his reasoning and asserted she was doing the best she could under the circumstances. Despite her own imminent departure from the UK, she continued to maintain the contact she had with Rob as often as she could, whilst keeping up with the demands of her other commitments, including her full-time job.

She reminisced back to the time they had first begun planning for Rob's trip, prior to meeting in Bali. They had concluded the seven and a half months they had waited to be together following their holiday in Bali had proved very difficult for them to cope with, even though they were still very much a couple, there had been occasions their relationship had become strained, due to the distance between them. At times they felt especially lonely having spent only a few days together since they had first met. The original plan had been for Rob to wait until she had arrived in Australia March 2017, after their holiday in Bali.
With Christmas around the corner Rob's daughters had expressed a preference to spend it with their Mother Loryn that year.

Rob was deeply affected by their decision not to spend Christmas with him and facing the reality he would be spending Christmas alone, he confessed his upset at their decision. She suggested he contacted his friend Treen who he regarded as a sister. Treen had been possibly the only supporter of their relationship; unfortunately Treen had made plans to spend the Christmas holidays away and would not be able to oblige Rob's request to spend Christmas with him. She could not bear the thought of him spending Christmas alone, especially with Christmas being such an important occasion for him. She thought about the money she needed to save before her trip and concluded that she would be okay financially because Hita had secured a job for her once she arrived. As much as she needed the money she felt she would a lot happier if she was able to see Rob on at least a couple of occasions prior to moving to Australia it would kills two birds with one stone and Rob would not have to spend Christmas alone.

She worked tirelessly in executing their renewed plans, only to have to change them again a few days later. Rob had informed his daughters of his plans to spend Christmas with her in the UK and then all hell broke loose. Rob's daughters Trista and Melissa were most upset he would not be in Australia for Christmas and manipulated him in to thinking he was being selfish, after being worn down by them following endless discussions and a change of heart, and agreed to spend part of Christmas Day with him. Rob agreed to discuss postponing the holiday until a couple of days after Christmas and celebrate the New Year in the UK instead, providing she was in agreement with the new arrangements.

Initially she was upset at the suggestion to postpone the dates the whole reason for Rob's trip to England had been borne out of Trista and Melissa's dysfunction. It had been left to her to put a plan in place for Rob due to their protests of not wanting to include their Father in their plans in Christmas. She was adamant she would not change her mind concerning the dates, especially as she was funding the trip, Rob reasoned with her stating that his children were wrong with the way they had handled things, however it would probably be the last Christmas with them, once she arrived in Australia and pleaded with her to change her mind and move the dates two days. Knowing how much it meant to him is the only reason why she agreed to it understanding how much it meant to him and she did not want to get in the way of that Rob had suffered enough with his daughter's and she would do anything to make him happy; by agreeing to the new dates only deepened the resentment she already held towards his children.

She found it remarkable the contrast in Rob's attitude towards his trip to England, from the on start of their relationship he had made it clear that he had no interest in visiting England, due to the distance and the cold weather, neither appealed to him. Rob did not think he could travel on a plane for up to twenty-four hours and certainly did not relish the idea of experiencing the cold weather; climates he was not used to.

Whenever she attempted to broach the subject with him it did not end well, at times Rob was completely non-committal about the idea and on other occasions he would quickly change the subject just to validate his detest. For her it was about killing two birds with one stone whereby possible, with their respective countries being so far away she was keen to forge ahead with plans, of him visiting her birth country and getting to know more about her as a person, her lifestyle and culture. She was keen to get plans in place, whereas Rob was unable to think beyond their plans for Bali, however since that holiday Rob had suggested going to England now he could not wait to visit, especially as she would be paying for the trip. In hindsight she fully understood his reservations, she did not blame Rob for having reservations she had lived in England all her life and was tired of the unpredictable British weather and the one aspect she looked forward to was the warmer climates she would be experiencing in weeks to come.

So far her plans to leave the U.K were forging ahead quite smoothly at times too smoothly, it seemed surreal. Despite the year she had prepared for her move to Australia, she believed it was an integral part of the Lord's divine plans for her, she deserved this opportunity she had dedicated her entire life to raising her daughter as a single parent and felt the possibility of a new start was some form of reward for all the personal sacrifices she had endured combined with the added encouragement she received from both Hita and Rob leading up to the big move. As the time drew nearer for her own departure she questioned whether the offer to move to Australia was within her best interests, she put it down to nerves. She trusted Hita and Rob explicitly in the past she had politely turned down offers from family members based in the United States, they had offered similar openings when Tia was just a baby, she could not bear the thought of being separated from her young daughter at the time and even though the opportunity was tempting, being a Mother to Tia was more important to her.

Her trip to Australia had come at the right time for her, although she was nervous about uprooting her life to the other side of the world, did not have the heart to back now, and what else did she have to lose, she believed she had exhausted all her options in the UK and at the very least she was no longer happy with her life here, something was missing the man she loved was anxiously waiting for her and she did not want to let anyone down, there were so many relying on her to make the trip, she shuddered at the effects of the possible aftermath if she did not go through with it, at most she would feel guilty and it would do irrepressible damage to her twenty year friendship she had with Hita which was so important to her. This was the third time Hita had asked her to make the move during the fourteen years she had been living there, if she didn't take up the offer now she doubted the offer would be extended again and she certainly did not want to spend a lifetime speculating over another missed opportunity, or run the risk of ruining her relationship with Rob.

Rob's upcoming trip to the UK and Holland was all they mainly discussed, added with their excitement about seeing each other again. She welcomed Rob's enthusiasm and they would talk extensively about the history they would be creating by making the trip, including the lifetime memories. No one else in his family had ever made it to Holland before, she felt proud knowing she was instrumental in making this trip possible for him as well as the tales he would be able to tell his grandchildren in years to come. The only concern Rob held until he left Australia was the duration of the flight.

He admitted he was concerned about whether he would be able to withstand the length of the journey. Rob had since developed a limp which had been causing him unbearable pain, he was fully apologetic of his condition and blamed the Gout he suffered being more aggressive than it had been in the past; he also developed Rheumatoid Arthritis and was advised the combination of both conditions was wreaking havoc on his wellbeing, Rob was an active outdoors man and worried if the condition worsened how much it would affect his agility. She expressed her concerns about his diet, Rob was of a stocky build and she felt the strain of his weight may add to his lack of mobility and worried the longer the limp may become permanent. Despite how poorly he felt Rob was able to look on the bright side and noted that every part of the journey would be worth it if it meant they would be able to spend time together.

The day had finally arrived for Rob's visit to the UK, leading up to this point she had worked tirelessly ensuring every part of her home had been spring cleaned prior to his arrival. She had even gone to the extent of personally redecorating her bedroom herself to make sure it was comfortable enough for him. Although she had tidied the garden with it being winter, she felt no desire to do much more to it before Rob arrived. Gardening as a rule was not her expertise, secretly she hoped Rob would help her to attend to it with any down time they had. She made sure Rob was updated on all her efforts to welcome him to England, although he was excited to see her and impressed with her efforts, he felt guilty of the efforts she had made and often express she was doing too much to accommodate him, especially with her own move to Australia coming up. However she insisted it needed to be done; the endeavours she made had noticeably affected her health, she had suffered with high blood pressure, chest pains and fatigue and at best she had been surviving on just four hours sleep per night. She put it down to the stress of her preparing for Rob's arrival as well as her own life in Australia.

Prior to boarding his flight Rob felt nervous about his visit and worried whether Tia would like him in person. During the time they had been together Tia and Rob had managed to forge a good friendship and would often spend time winding each other up either on the phone or via FaceTime. Rob had never really shown much interest in what her home was like now that he was on his way he was intrigued with what it was like and did his best to imagine the layout of it. Rob's flight was scheduled to arrive at Heathrow at twenty past eight that morning; she had struggled to sleep due to the excitement of his visit. She had been awake since three thirty and gave the house a quick once over, she had also cooked the night before to ensure that lunch would be ready by the time they returned home and it would allow her more time to spend with him without any interruptions.

She arrived at Heathrow airport at seven thirty and remembered during the journey there had been a lot of dense Fog along the way and wondered whether it had been severe enough to cause his flight to be delayed. She had been monitoring his flights online since he had first boarded and there had been no information announced regarding any expected delays. After checking the flight monitor to confirm there were no sudden updates she felt there was no reason to be concerned and waited opposite the arrival gates, so they would be able to see each other as soon as he entered the area. She had been waiting for this moment for a while; whilst she waited patiently for his plane to land she wondered how he felt about her.

Whenever they spoke on the phone she had no doubts that he still crazy about her. The few extra pounds she was carrying that she had not been able to lose, were rather noticeable. Although she looked good for her age and she had kept up with the power walking, she had not given herself enough time to lose the extra pounds as she would have liked, due to all the her other responsibilities and the recent bouts of illness. She pondered whether Rob would be comfortable at hers, although her household was quite laid back her plans to complete the redecorating and refurbishing had been put on hold since her initial return from Australia. Prior to Hita's invitation she had been in the early throws of completing it with plans to complete when she returned. Now that her plans had changed she had basically abandoned ship, it did not make any financial sense to finish it. After many discussions regarding the home after she left, they had decided that it would be unfair for Tia to put her life on hold for twelve months, just to find out whether her mum would be returning to the UK. Tia was keen to take the refurbishing on as a new project and had different ideas than what she had been planning, more importantly she needed the finance she would have invested to return to Australia, rather than spend it on the home she would not be around to enjoy.

With the new plans firmly in place, Tia had designs on moving in to the master bedroom and all her existing furniture would either be sold or given to Charity. Her prospects for the future were a daunting thought, What if the trip did not go according to plan? What if she had a change of heart when she got there? She quickly dispelled the negative thoughts that were attempting to torment her. She felt it unfair to keep Tia in limbo whilst she carried on with life overseas, Tia had a right to carve out a new life for herself, everything was changing and she needed to accept the changes when they presented themselves. She would only be able to accommodate her personal belongings such as her clothing and personal artefacts.

Gladys, a colleague from work, had advised her not to leave too many items behind, she explained that to do so, would not be a full commitment towards her future, but rather a half measure as if she was holding on to things back in the UK as a 'just in case measure'. Gladys explained the things from her past life could not be brought in to her new life and to do so would hinder the process. She agreed with Gladys wholeheartedly the whole purpose of the journey was to start a new life, holding on to old furniture that would have been replaced as a result of the renovations, were not part of the long term plans for her future. From the endless discussions she had leading up to the move, Rob and Hita were of the opinion she should not think about returning to the UK on a full-time basis and that her future would be based in Australia going forward.

An hour had almost gone by and there had been no sign of Rob or an update provided regarding his flight. A lot of the later flights that were scheduled had been updated on the display boards. She struggled with either going to make enquiries with a member of staff regarding the flight; however she did not want to leave where she was standing just in case she missed him. By now her feet were aching and she was in need of a hot drink to keep her warm in the chilly surroundings. She walked over to the Starbucks that was situated just behind where she stood and ordered a Latte; she seated herself inside where she was able to view display boards and Arrival's gate simultaneously. Half an hour later and there was still no sign of Rob.

She started to become quite anxious and wondered why the information board had not yet provided an update. All sorts of concerns now plagued her mind, she wondered whether he had suffered any illness during the flight and had been unable to continue the journey. Unlike her own trip to Australia she had made two stops en route. Rob flight had only one stop-off in Abu Dhabi and they had spoken when he had arrived there, right up until he went to board the last flight and there had been no problems, in fact Rob had enjoyed it. There were no airport staff members around for her to speak with. She asked herself whether the delay was a sign of things to come and even began a mental conversation with God to ascertain why these sorts of unexplained occurrences always happened to her. Almost half an hour later the arrival doors automatically swung open and Rob entered larger than life beaming the biggest smile, whilst scouting the crowds looking for her. In typical lumber jack fashion Rob carried his luggage bag perched on his shoulder and held his red checked overcoat and rucksack in his other hand.

At the sight of him she makes her way over in his direction, Rob had not seen her yet as she manoeuvred through the small crowd towards him. She was only a few steps away when Rob spotted her edging towards him, with his arms outstretched they embraced each other a few times, welcoming him to Britain and snuggled in to his arms, they were finally reunited again. Rob later explained the flight had been delayed been due to the fog; the plane had been forced to circle around the airport several times before receiving clearance to land. Any doubts she may have had about Rob's visit up until then quickly diminished, they were together again and that was all they had wanted.

They exited the airport homeward bound and excitedly discussed their plans during his stay. After they arrived home she gave him a guided tour of her place. Tia was not due to arrive home until later that afternoon; she quickly settled him in with a much needed shower after travelling for twenty-four hours and organised the lunch she had pre-prepared for him the night before and something to drink whilst she unpacked his belongings into the empty wardrobe and chest of drawers she had arranged to him. Rob felt more than comfortable at her place even though it was a lot smaller in comparison to what he was used to, he really liked it and he commented it was a lot larger than he had imagined. Rob was no stranger to the English property programmes he watched in Australia and often stated he could not understand why property prices in the UK were so exorbitant, some he had seen on the programmes retailed well in excess of a million pounds, for properties he described as no larger than matchboxes.

They spent the first few days visiting all the London major attractions, including Buckingham Palace, Westminster Abbey, Tower Bridge, The West End, Harrods, Covent Garden, Chinatown, Leicester Square and the likes; they even rode the Emirates Cable

Cars an activity she had never done before, in between their pursuits they found plenty of time to stop off and pub-crawl, which Rob found most enjoyable sampling the various beers available even though he was not fond of most that he tasted, the highlight for her so far had been them seeing in the New Year together, watching the fireworks whilst toasting in the New Year and drinking champagne. The last time she had been to see the London fireworks was more than twenty-four years ago, after having her daughter she preferred to watch it on screen and could not be asked with the hassle of trudging through the crowds for the perpetual task of the mammoth journey home after dark. She had found it a particularly poignant moment and believed it would be the last time she would ever see the fireworks in person again.

Since his arrival Rob had naturally embraced every aspect of London and its lifestyle and became quite familiar with the area, he thoroughly enjoyed his time there, but surmised he was a country man and did not think he could live in a city on a permanent basis. Although the temperatures were in their minuses and often accompanied by a dusting of snow or heavy rainfall, she thought it was remarkable how he was able to acclimatise to the freezing climates of London more so than its inhabitants, considering he was only used to warm climates. Melbourne was noted for having similar weather to the UK; however the temperatures were dramatically warmer and resembled the Tropics whatever the season, even during their winters there were many days that were relatively warmer than even the UK's hottest days. Rob was so unaffected by the UK's cool temperatures he would often carry his outwear, rather than wear it and regularly joked about the British being pansies for not being able to stand the harsh British weather even though they had plenty of occasions to get used to it.

A week later they visited their local Flight Centre and booked a four night stay in Holland. The flight and accommodation was a lot more expensive than they had anticipated, however it would be their first flight together and was considered an important part of the agenda during Rob's European tour. They were due to leave within the next two days and Rob would finally be able to visit the actual birthplaces of his late Dutch parents. They arrived at Gatwick Airport three hours prior to their flight which was not due to depart until eleven-thirty that morning. This would mean they did not have to rush and it would give them a chance to eat breakfast prior to boarding. They were really excited about their first excursion, where they would be able to experience every aspect of the trip simultaneously.

After breakfast they made their way to check-in their luggage, during the search in the customs area they were was approached by Airport security and asked to open their bags as a precautionary measure. With her search completed she secured her hand luggage and made her way over to where Rob was standing whilst still undergoing his search. To her dismay she noted the Operative was chastising Rob whose hand luggage had virtually been completely emptied on to the counter in between them. The operative explained that certain items he had travelled with exceeded the hundred millilitre allowance that could be taken on board the aircraft. She quickly averted her eyes to some of the products the operative had been referring to which included a large can of Rexona antiperspirant, a bottle of shaving cream and other personal toiletries, as she returned her attention back to the operative she he had hold of a bottle of KY jelly that he continuously waved around on show as he continued talking.

Rob had been given the option of either discarding the items or storing the items in the aircrafts holdall. Her mouth dropped open in shock, Rob had purchased the item soon after his arrival in London in the prerequisite they might require it, having been apart for a three and a half months. Rob thought the purchase was thoughtful, although they had not used it. She was in disbelieve the object was now in the hands of security personnel in one of the most highly sensitive and public of places possible. Underneath her tanned skin she blushed heavily she could feel her blood vessels tingling in the pit of her stomach. She was embarrassed by the events taking place as the security guard continued to wave the product and totally oblivious.

She averted her attention between Rob and the security guard wishing she could put an immediate end to the situation, not wanting to explore the possibility of the other travellers standing nearby, being aware of what was happening with them. Rob had been given a choice to make and instead of doing so, he chose to entertain a deeper discussion with the operative by attempting to explain away the mistake of bringing the offending items. Rob seemed completely unaware of the KY Jelly on display and was oblivious to her feelings, whilst he continued with his explanation regarding the weight allowance permitted; he finally made a decision not to discard the items, and agreed to check-in his hand luggage in to the hole as advised. The security official informed to do so, he would be required to leave the security area and return to the main part of the airport and check-in the hand luggage by an automatic scanner which located on the floor below and then return to the security area to be rechecked-in as passengers. Rob stated he did not want to check-in a second time and to her dismay, he proposed she should take the offending items add them to her hand-luggage, check-in the bag and then return to meet him in the waiting area of the airport after being rechecked-in.

Her immediate reaction upon hearing his suggestion was to pass him a disapproving look and overrode his suggestion by insisting they check the bag in together. This was a side to Rob she did had not witnessed before and hoped she never encountered again, for a moment she wondered where the gentleman she knew had disappeared to, Rob mostly referred to them as a team, however she was yet to see any examples of team spirit during this particular situation. They made their way back through the automated check-in area; by now they were both frustrated and continued to bicker amongst each other. She informed him about her upset regarding the KY Jelly he had chosen to accompany them on their travels, whilst Rob continued relaying a string of excuses in his defence ranging from he had not realised he had packed the KY Jelly and although he able to admit to his mistake, he also felt she was overacting to the situation overall and stated it was not the end of the world. The automatic check-in process turned out to be more arduous than they hand anticipated and with the assistance of a reluctant operative nearby they checked in the hand luggage and even managed to evade the steep levy fee of thirty-eight pounds to their relief.

As they took their seats on board the cramped Easy Jet aircraft, she secured herself in to her station, checked Rob was okay and soon drifted off fast asleep almost for the entire flight. An hour and a half later, she felt herself being nudged awake by Rob, as she opened her eyes reluctantly, she heard him whisper, "Hey you! Remember me?" She looked up at him and smiled as she leaned in to him for a cuddle.

As they lined up with the other passengers to exit the plane, she braced herself for the minus five Siberian winter temperatures the pilot had mentioned prior to their flight landing. She found the temperatures unbearable encompassed with the added brisk winds and quickly resorted to finding her human radiator as she snuggled in to Rob's arms as they entered inside the terminal. They had twin room booked for them at the Tulip Inn Hotel situated in the Amsterdam's main centre, after obtaining the details of locating the hotel from the airport information desk; they made their way to the train station adjacent. The train journey would be a total of an hour and a half in to Amsterdam with the hotel situated ten minutes away. They thought it would be sensible to use the bathroom before starting the journey and arranged to meet up outside when they were finished. She could not have been gone any longer than ten minutes before leaving the bathroom to meet Rob, as she exited and ventured outside to find him. Rob was speaking to a train attendant as she walked over towards him whilst doing so she noticed Rob had a ghastly look on his face, he returned her intrigued look and literally took off and began running away from her in the opposite direction and without any attempt to explain what the emergency was, and what was even more apparent was that Rob's limp, that was caused by severe Gout and Rheumatoid Arthritis symptoms that he had continuously complained about had all but vanished. The expression on her face although she was not privy to seeing it, could only be described as utter disbelief.

As Rob sprinted around the corner and almost out of sight it dawned on her that he was running in the direction of an unsuspecting blonde hair and blue eyed female who was standing unawares with her back to him. As Rob approached her another train attendant yelled out to him that whatever the problem had been, all was okay and that his previous efforts were no longer required and the issue was all in hand.   Rob stopped dead in the middle of his tracks and returned to the bathroom area, looking quite sheepish and despaired with his limp back in tow. As he approached her she was by now seething and made her feelings quite clear, she cited she had no problem with him helping a damsel in distress; she expected that of him, but to know they were in a foreign place where neither of them knew where the hell they were exactly, did not bode well with her. She asked him to explain the absent limp having witnessed his best Usain Bolt impression, she had never seen him move so spritely and suggested his limp only appeared to be present whenever they were together.

She was disappointed in the way Rob had handled things, although he acknowledged her frustrations and excused his behaviour maintaining he had not been given any time to explain things prior to reacting due to the circumstances. The female passenger had left her mobile and a train operative had found it and had planned on reuniting it with its owner, but Rob had insisted on doing his job for him, even and had been prevented from doing so, whilst the train attendant handled the matter themselves. She was not impressed with Rob's actions, although she understood his reasons; overall she felt it was none of his business, considering he had not actually found the lost item himself, combined with the bitter winter temperatures falling even lower she was really upset, cold, tired and hungry and was not in the mood to be agreeable with the absurdity she had just witnessed. Unable to reach any medium between them they spent the entire train journey both in complete silence and deep in their own thoughts, until they arrived at the hotel.

As they boarded the lift to the first floor of the hotel, they found themselves having to manoeuver a set of spiral staircases to reach the Mezzanine level. Rob with his limp back in full force found the climb even more challenging than she had. The appearance of the hotel room they had booked only added to the misery of their despondent mood. Having completed what could only be described as an assault course to locate the hotel room; they stood firmly in agreement the appearance of the gloomy cramped room, did not reflect the pictures they had seen online in anyway, overall the room was significantly below par and did not meet any of their expectations.

She felt the room itself was the most off putting she had ever seen and remarked if they remained in it during their time there and it would totally ruin the experience for both of them. The walls were covered in an old style white bubble paper reflective of the early seventies; it was in terrible condition and had turned in a discoloured grey, adorned with spots of chewing gum holding the worn bits together. The carpet consisted of a mustard and dark brown colour and incorporated a circular pattern where the two colours met in the middle; it had seen better days and appeared to be in keeping with the wallpaper. It was badly worn, dirty and sticky; the twin beds were levelled unevenly and pushed together. The bedding was made up of single sheets that contained lots of small holes and not considered fit for purpose by their standards. There was an old Victorian style wooden dressing table, again in keeping with the decadence of the other furnishings; it was centred in the narrowest part of the room opposite the bed, that area of the room was particularly dense and uninviting. An area of the room she had no plans of exploring.

She had spoken to Rob extensively about her scornfulness which she attributed to being a personal flaw in her character; nevertheless it was an imperfection she felt she could not help. Whilst she may have come from very humble beginnings, cleanliness and where she laid her head down at night was extremely important to her. Her disdain was very apparent she looked uncomfortable and felt a little relieved by what she considered to be the only decent aspect of the room being the brand new en suite. Rob apologised for the poor appearance of the room and offered to speak with the reception desk first thing the following morning about moving to alternative room as quickly as possible. It was by now the early evening and quite dark outside, the room had turned out to be an instant passion killer so they decided to get changed and have a look around for a bite to eat and a smoke. She had visited Holland several times in the past, and whenever she visited she had thoroughly enjoyed it, she admired the social and carefree culture of Dutch. Her eldest brother Howard, niece Yasmin and friend Sheldon all lived there and she hoped to be able to meet up with them during their stay so they could introduce Rob to them.

Amsterdam had not changed much since her last visit four years before, irrespective of when she visited, she always found it damp, busy and terribly cold. Outside the hotel they walked along the cobbled streets behind the other tourists taking in the sites, as they made a decision of where the best place was to get some smokes. The Bulldog Lounge was always busy and that evening was no different, with a staunch poignant mix of marijuana circulating the air, Rob went up to the counter and unbeknown to her purchased four pre-rolled reefers, two of which contained just the natural herb. With a lack of seating available inside the venue they soon found a vacant corner located nearby. Rob lit the first smoke he had chosen to sample one of the stronger types and as he inhaled it, he immediately started spluttering as his lungs gave out, the reefer smelt strong and she put the affect it had on Rob down to its potency, rather than the reefer being made without tobacco.

Rob was still coughing uncontrollably as he puffed on it a second time, other patrons inside the venue had also noticed him coughing, another customer who had just been served commented in jest that the smoke must be good, due to the affects it was having on him. Rob passed it to her unable to contain his cough; she inhaled her drag deeply and began spluttering herself exactly as he had done as she tried to exhale the fumes to Rob's own amusement. They puffed and passed the reefer back to one another until it was finished, failing to stifle their coughs in between. After twenty minutes they decided to browse the streets for a light bite to eat and ventured down one of the side streets, as they turned in to the road they had begun heading down, she noticed two young black males walking towards them, there was something about them she found unscrupulous, they were talking and laughing amongst themselves, yet both men stared constantly at her as they did so. She was unable to hear what they were saying, but believed they were Dutch she worried with Rob limping beside her whether they were about to become targets. As they passed by the culprits, she felt her right ass cheek become uncomfortably hot and quickly ascertained, she had just been slapped hard on the arse by one of the men, so much so the force from the blow had penetrated her leather trousers, leaving quite a noticeable sting. She could not believe what had happened to her, not only had she been violated by a complete stranger, the incident had gone unnoticed by Rob and now she had the added problem of whether to inform Rob. She felt compelled to tell him, they had always been so open and trusting with each other, but she felt nervous about his reaction. Rob was a massive character and she had concerns over how he would cope with being told. She did not want him to confront those responsible under any circumstances, not only would he be outnumbered she did not want any harm to come to him and recalled Rob telling her about the breakdown of his marriage four years ago.

Rob's ex-wife Loryn had a reputation for being an awful drunk and unable to handle her drink once fully inebriated. Rob had complained to her, about previous occasions where Loryn had embarrassed herself and her family because of it, and several of those occasions involved Rob having to drag her home from their local pub. During one particular occurrence Loryn had returned home from a night out with friends and appeared quite distressed and feeling sorry for herself. Loryn informed Rob her drink had been spiked and maintained she had been date-raped. Admittedly, at the time Rob had first mentioned it to her, she immediately noticed red flags; the story Rob had recalled appeared to be quite sketchy, incomplete and in part made very little sense.

Loryn had been adamant about not reporting the incident to the police and was unwilling to make a statement, or receive counselling. Giving her the impression if this had been a genuine incident, why had she refused to seek help at the time. She refrained from discussing her opinion with Rob, in her mind the incident had occurred four years ago, way before her time and a part of their history that ultimately had nothing to do with her. Rob maintained he had been accepting of the situation and had done his best to support his ex-wife; however he felt his efforts were never reciprocated and a result of which had put a detrimental strain on their marriage. After four years of just going through the motions for the sake of the children, Rob had grown tired of the situation and they agreed to call time on their thirty year marriage and as a result had separated.

She looked over her shoulder and could see the offenders responsible for violating her laughing in amusement as they disappeared around the corner; she believed this moment was a good time as any to speak to Rob about the incident. Rob's reaction to the news was depictive of his character. Rob stopped dead fast in the middle of the street where they had been walking and demanded to know where the culprits were. With the culprits out of sight, she was able to reassure him that it was not worth the hassle. Although her feelings were hurt there was no permanent damage done, she would eventually get over it. Rob apologised to her for the incident and felt remorseful he had been unable to protect her during her time of need.

The remainder of the holiday went accordingly without any further glitches; the hotel had kindly upgraded them to an attic suite located on the seventh floor. The hotel suite was in absolute contrast to the first room they had been allocated, it came complete with a walk-in shower, decorated in a contemporary bricked style, the room had a double-bed, even though it had been dressed in single sheets, these particular bed sheets smelt fresh and clean and came without moth holes. Owing to the disappointment of the previous room they had spent the night in, they felt as if they had struck gold with the updated suite.

The following day they set off early for breakfast en-route to Leeuwarden to visit Rob's Mother's birthplace. The train ride was a two hour journey, including a couple of train transfers in between. By the time they had arrived in Leeuwarden the temperatures were a bitter minus nine and it was snowing quite heavily. Leeuwarden was an old rural city, aligned with cobbled streets, traditional pubs and local eateries. As they headed towards the main town centre they stopped off at an outside bakery stall, where Rob sampled and reminisced over two 'Oliebollen' Dutch Doughnuts in between gulps. Rob thanked her for being such a good sport in accompanying him on this part of the holiday, knowing how much the trip meant to him, she responded it was her pleasure to witness him enjoying himself, whilst completing his ancestral journey. Leeuwarden was a small city and once they had taken a good look around, they settled for a few drinks in a pub close to the train station and shared their reasons for visiting the town with the barman and a couple of the local patrons.

A day later they visited Rotterdam to visit Rob's Father's birthplace, although the weather was still very chilly, it was a lot more pleasant than it had been when they had visited Leeuwarden the day before. Rotterdam denoted a tone of strict formality in comparison and was engulfed with lots of architecture and corporate buildings. It was one of the cleanest parts of the country they had visited so far and felt the stately city appealed to her more than Leeuwarden. Rob had forgotten to travel with any documentation concerning his parents, despite this they tried their chances at the local Town Hall attempting to ascertain any information, regarding possible graveyards they could visit. Unfortunately they were only able to complete a general search which proved futile without the necessary documentation.

Rob was upset with himself for not being better prepared, however she was able to reassure him that concerning the plans they had made between them for the future; whenever they visited England thereafter, they could always return with the necessary paperwork. During his visit to Holland Rob had developed a real affinity with the Netherlands and could relate to a lot of the history and cultural aspects it offered. Howard and Sheldon were not available at short notice to meet them as they were both busy, they were disappointed because they had been unable to forewarn them of their visit beforehand, she had hoped meeting up with them would have been simple to organise once they arrived, however it was not meant to be and she would not be able to see Howard before she departed for Australia.

With the remaining time they had left before returning to England, they spent it visiting some of the main attractions, including the Ice Bar, the Sex Museum and the infamous Red Light district which they did a few times. There was something she found fondly enthralling about it, she found the Red Light District intriguing and unlike any other city she visited. One of the most humorous occasions for them had been visiting the Red Light District during the last day of their stay. With only four days in Holland they had compressed lots of activities in to the days they spent there. To fit it all in, entailed waking up at the crack of dawn and spending the days cramming in as many pursuits as possible and the final day of the trip would be no different. They awoke early, packed their belongings and checked out of the hotel, with only four hours remaining, prior to returning to the airport they spent the rest of the time they had left completing last minute activities. The Tulip Inn Hotel staff had kindly offered to store their luggage, until they were ready to return to the UK. Rob asked her if there was anything she wanted to do prior to leaving Amsterdam, she suggested they revisited the Red Light District if he had no better suggestions, even though it was the early hours of the morning she suggested there were parts of the District they had not seen yet and she guaranteed him, the girls who worked in the mornings were cut from a very different cloth from the girls they had seen previously at night.

They strolled around the wet cobbled streets on the lookout for the illuminated red lights, to help identify the few scantily-clad working girls, sat behind the windows at that time of the morning. After strolling around the winding streets they soon became weary and decided to walk down one another lane before calling it a day. They settled on a small cobbled side road with no more than four full length windows on either side of the pavement, all of the windows were vacant except the last window situated at the end of the very end of street. She walked on ahead, in front of Rob as she passed the window at the end she noticed one of the ladies she had been describing to Rob earlier. As Rob ventured up to the window behind her, she was already a few steps ahead and stopped on the other side of the window opening, slightly out of view of the prostitute seated inside.

Rob walked up to the centre of the window and stood directly in front of it taking in the view inside, whilst doing so the lady of the night yelled at him in a piercing voice and told him in no uncertain terms to "eff off." Throughout the ordeal Rob remained completely composed and following a short pause, Rob sarcastically thanked her before continuing on his way. They concluded she lacked the required customer service skills required for her profession and laughed off the incident. With the time remaining Rob decided on a tattoo of the Dutch and Australian flags intertwined on his right inner forearm. They also visited the Ice Bar, and stacked up on Rob's childhood favourites, Almond Tarts and Kalfsvleeskrokets. Overall the trip had been a huge success; Rob had enjoyed Amsterdam so much it was a trip he planned to revisit whenever he could.

Their return flight to London had gone smoothly, until they arrived in London. They returned to the UK in the midst of a train strike, which meant actually getting back home would be somewhat of a mission, yet not impossible. They had not had much downtime whilst being in Holland and their return flight had been a late one. Upon entering Gatwick train station at seven in the evening, the platforms were awash with other stranded passengers, desperately trying to organise alternative routes home via the limited amount of trains laid on. They had not prepared themselves for the pandemonium they were about to ensue and were both feeling quite exhausted and just wanting to get back to the normality of home as quickly as possible. By now she felt particularly drained and quite nauseous from the trip, with it being late evening and still being quite away from home they could not have chosen a worst day to travel back from the Netherlands.

They had been waiting in line for train tickets for some time before it was their turn to be served by the train operative, as she approached the counter she was feeling somewhat out of sorts and mistakenly requested train tickets from her local train station, rather than Gatwick Train station where they were currently located, with all the delays and chaos surrounding them, it took her a while to register they would require train tickets from Gatwick to their local train station. The ticket attendant and Rob sensed her turmoil and right on cue they laughed in hysterics, after reminding her she was still at Gatwick airport and that she it would take her at least three hours to walk home.

With only a week remaining before Rob's departure there were a couple of more items on Rob's bucket list he wanted to complete before leaving. Rob was keen to meet with her Dad and sister-in-law Carlita. She was nervous about introducing Rob to her Dad, she was the apple of her Father's eye and they were exceptionally close. She felt compromised about introducing Rob to her Dad and had it not been for her leaving the country in a few weeks, she would certainly have delayed the meeting. The only partner she had ever officially introduced to her Father was Tia's Father twenty-four years ago, she had never consider anyone else worthy of ever meeting her Father, in fact her Dad had only met Grim by accident. Overall she felt Rob meeting with her Dad would be the right thing to do and Rob had been able to convince her that the meeting was also important to him and believed it would be the decent thing to do under the circumstances. The meeting went better than she had expected, her Father had been full of the usual charm and welcomed Rob in to the family, whilst Rob did everything possible to reassure her Father how much he loved his daughter and that he would take excellent care of her when she arrived in Australia.

A couple of days prior to Rob's departure Carlita visited to meet Rob, Carlita expressed to Rob how much her Sister-In-Law meant to her and that she felt it was only right to meet the person responsible for taking her away from her loved ones. Rob and Carlita got on exceptionally well; she noticed how happy they were together and commented on hoping to find a love like theirs one day. They invited Carlita to visit them in Australia once they were settled. A short time after Rob made his excuses and decided to pop to the shops, allowing them some quality time together. Carlita had separated from her younger brother four years before and they had been as close as sisters from the first time they met. Twenty years later, Carlita had blessed her with two nieces and nephews whom she adored. Following their split her brother was completely out of the picture, neither of them ever heard from him, yet their relationship had continued to flourish over the years. She doted on her nieces and nephews and due to her brother's absence, she felt a sense of duty to remain a permanent fixture in their lives. With Rob out of the way Carlita made no hesitation in offering her opinion. Carlita assured her she was making the right decision in leaving the UK to be with Rob, not only did she deserve to be happy she could tell how much Rob adored her.

Rob would be leaving for Australia the following day and she had mixed emotions about his departure; although she would be joining him in five weeks she would really miss having him around. It was crunch time and the focus for her needed to be entirely on her move to Australia. She worried whether she would be able to get everything done with the small amount of time she had before she was due to leave. With hindsight she wished she had arranged for Rob to come over to England later or at least until she actually left the country, so they could travel together and he would be there to support her when the time came for her to leave Tia. In all honesty it was probably better the way it had been planned, as well as the time she had remaining, she would also need to schedule in time to say her final farewells to family and friends. She had only conveyed her future plans to her nearest and dearest. Her decision to leave had been difficult enough initially and had involved fourteen months of meticulous planning, involving others at that stage would have just added more stress and would have overly complicated matters for her. The time was right for her to pursue this journey; Hita had first invited her to Australia over ten years ago and had been exceedingly patient in waiting for her to finally make the move.

She had a prestigious role as a Senior Executive Assistant to the Acting CEO of her local hospital, however due to it being a Charity the position came without the luxurious benefits and competitive remunerations other EA's were offered in the private sector, having made a conscious decision to leave the private sector due to the instability of the market at that time. Although she enjoyed the role and was exceptional at it, the recent changes within the National Health Service had made her work environment depressing and at times unbearable to work in, due to the constant pay cuts and organisational restructures, the future of her role was still undecided and the uncertainty of it all left very little light at the end of the tunnel in terms of promotion or remuneration increase.

Rob had picked up on her concerns regarding his leaving and had noticed the depressed change in her demeanour. He confessed he felt the same about her and for the first time he realised how torn and apprehensive she may be feeling about leaving the country to start a new life, as well as the difficulties of leaving her daughter behind. He has concerns of his own and feared when the time came for her own departure, she would be unable to go through with it and wished he was able to stay till then to make her leaving easier. She did not want Rob's last day in England to end on a depressing note, it was not the end of the world and whilst she was not ready for him to return to Australia, they would be reunited within a few weeks.

She contacted Hita to remind her of Rob's departure the following morning and that she planned to purchase her own ticket to Australia thereafter and wanted to confirm that she all was okay to book the plane ticket as planned. Hita confirmed their plans were still very much on and that they couldn't wait to see her and she was looking forward to them working on her business together. Rob felt relieved by Hita's confirmation it lessened any concerns he first had and now he was just as excited about returning to Australia to get things in place for her when she arrived. With her departure now finalised, she thought back to the day fourteen months ago, when she had first agreed to go, there were times her departure seemed so far away back then, suddenly the day had crept up on her all of a sudden with just only a month to go until she left, now she wished she had given herself more time to prepare.

The last week of work was more difficult that she had anticipated, she had not informed her colleagues regarding her intentions to take a sabbatical; it had not been easy getting the time off authorised, although her Line Manager had agreed the time off a year before, another colleague had also requested a sabbatical immediately after her which had been approved and in turn her original request had been denied. With a twist of faith she appealed the decision and included supporting evidence and the assistance from a Chief Directorate who supported her decision. The request for leave was eventually finalised and approved and the former colleagues request for a career break was revoked. The offended colleague later resigned under condition she would not appeal the decision, if the Hospital obliged to continue to pay remunerations for the next quarter. She would have preferred a similar arrangement as her former colleague, however she had faithfully promised her Father she would secure the sabbatical, before leaving for Australia. The handling of the sabbatical by her employers had taken over a year to arrange and had caused her nothing but unnecessary grief whenever a follow-up was required, due to the overhaul of the department. She would often complain to both her Father and Rob about the obstacles she faced whenever she attempted to finalise the decision. Rob did not feel the stress was worth it, he had no intentions of her ever returning to the post once she officially left, he felt the hassle for her was needless and implied she should not be so forthcoming with her Father, by confirming the career break had been finalised even if it had not been. She had never been dishonest to her Father before and had no intentions of starting now, her Dad only wanted what was best for his Daughter, although she had no reason to distrust Hita or Rob, she felt a compulsion to finalise the sabbatical before she travelled.

Sitting at her work station she carried out a quick search for cheap flights to Australia, a few of the offers looked relatively cheaper than the quotes she had received from her favourite carrier Royal Brunei Airlines, but contacted them anyway hoping they had cheaper flights available. Hita had advised her on purchasing an open-return ticket and of all the airlines Royal Brunei proved to the most expensive. Hita had suggested an open return ticket, because the Visitor's Visa she would be travelling on would offer the best flexibility to change the dates, because she would be required to check-in and check-out every quarter during the first year of her stay. She had visited Hita in Leicester a couple of months earlier and they had looked in to the possibility of travelling on a work visa, however Hita had decided against it, due to the cost of the visa being almost three thousand pounds, she felt that rather that put that as an expense through her business, it would be better to save that money and put it to better use.

She remembered her trip to Holland with Rob and contacted the Flight Centre online, requesting they contacted her back. Fiona from their Bristol branch contacted her immediately and promised to contact her the next day, after conducting a detailed search for flights availability. Fiona emailed her the next morning stating she was still looking in to it and would be in contact later that day with the details as requested. Thereafter Fiona had failed to make contact, she felt a little let down by Fiona and wondered what the hold-up was. Time was of the essence for her, she needed to organise the ticket as soon as possible so she could update Hita and Rob and they could make any necessary preparations their end before her arrival. It was important she got the flight information to them quickly to avoid inconveniencing any more than necessary. Another day passed by and Fiona had still not made contact. She was starting to believe Fiona was avoiding her, she had not responded to any of her phone calls or emails, after leaving a fourth message where Fiona blatantly refused to take the call, she had become upset at the mistreatment and unprofessional behaviour she now demonstrated. Feeling at a complete loss she contacted her local Flight Centre where she had booked the Holland trip with Rob direct and spoke with Nicole Schrieder and complained about the lack of response received from her colleague.

Nicole instantly recognised the urgency regarding her plans to leave the country within the next three weeks and promised to contact her with an update later that day. She felt it was doubtful Nicole would return her call because of Fiona's poor performance, however Nicole had been so professional and understanding she felt she had little choice but to go along with it. Within ten minutes Nicole had called back the ticket she offered was so cheap it was unrealistic, in addition to being a bargain, the ticket came with several added benefits including a free stay in a hotel to be redeemed at any time during travel and a three month Visitor's Visa among other benefits. She couldn't believe her luck and immediately settled payment to secure the flight. Nicole had not been impressed with her Fiona's lack of assistance and insisted on making a complaint on her behalf. As a result they formed a friendship and met up before she departed and kept in touch. Nicole knew Emerald well and stated she had lived there before with her ex-boyfriend at the time, she had only returned to the UK just six months before, owing to the relationship not working out and had since found love again with her new partner who worked as a Chef and was in the process of launching his own restaurant within the coming weeks.

During the run up to the end of the working week she felt a little sentimental about leaving her job. Abi her housekeeper had been making her feel guilty all week about her upcoming departure which resulted in lots of tears and upset or trying to convince her to change her mind about leaving. Deep down she felt she had outgrown her working environment and had no real ambitions about ever returning to her former role once she left, although the job was a cushy one the internal politics she felt were cumbersome and with the restructure being continually delayed after each deadline, meant the majority of staff had left in their droves and the new replacements were of a different era and preferred to remain out of sight and did not intermingle with the existing staff.

Gladys shared the office with her and was also due to end her contract a month later. Gladys had only started the job a year prior as a Senior Pathology Practitioner; she had taken a liking to her when she first started and went against protocol by requesting to work out of her office, rather than take the option to have her own. By doing so they had forged a close working relationship and friendship out of work. Gladys wholeheartedly supported her decision to go to Australia; she was very fond of Rob and they often spoke to each other via FaceTime. Gladys did however have reservations towards her friend Hita; even though they had never met she had difficulty comprehending their friendship, due to Hita's background.

As far as Gladys was concerned all Asians born in Kenya were nothing but racists and stated that in Kenya the Asians only ever used black people as slaves. She was startled when she had first heard it, it was so unlike Gladys to hold such strong views, she did her best to reassure Gladys about her twenty year friendship with Hita, citing that she knew the majority of Hita's family and maintained she had always been treated as the next best thing to family. Gladys was unconvinced and asked her to be careful, for some reason there was something about Hita she did not trust, but they agreed to disagree and in kind she invited both Abi and Gladys to visit her in Australia after she was settled. Abi hated flying but Gladys stated they would travel to Australia to visit her together.

With only ten days to go before she was due to leave the country she felt under immense pressure, she was in disbelief over the amount of things that remained outstanding that she needed to do, yet the time allotted to get all the tasks completed was diminishing at every turn. She still needed to pack her suitcase and fill an eighty kilogram box with the remainder of her personal possessions and arrange to have it shipped over to meet her at the other end. For the past year she had spent every day organising her departure, averaging on approximately four hours sleep, despite maintaining her daily responsibilities with only the support of her nearest and dearest, she had been able to complete the majority of what was required, however with the amount of items outstanding that still needed to be achieved and the ever increasing amount of time she had to do it all in, only further reinforced how life changing her move to Australia was and how many others would be affected by her decision.

She thought about Tia she had been so busy with the run up to the move, it suddenly dawned on her that for the entire time she would be away she would no longer be able to touch or kiss her daughter or see her daughter as she had been able to do every day for the past twenty-four years, the thought alone was almost unbearable to comprehend and made her sad and upset. She suddenly felt as if all the logistics and preparations in completing this mammoth task of the move, what was most important to her had been somewhat been the lesser consideration, when it should have been the other way around. It was then she made the decision to just take care of the necessary things and that with the assistance of Tia she would take of everything else after the move. Tia had also been oblivious of the time they had left together and immediately took the remaining time off work so they could spend the last few days together, they planned to do spend some quality time together with the family, and planned on creating some long lasting memories, including small intimate leaving party at one of their favourite hangouts they were known to frequent before she left.

With only seven days before her departure date due everything she could have hoped to go wrong certainly did its best to do so. It seemed to be the week for a succession of unexpected surprises, neither of which were welcomed. Deep down she was so excited by the prospect of starting her new life in Australia, however her heart was heavy with all she would be leaving behind, it was all she had ever known, once she arrived in Australia she would be in the land of unknown territory, she would be looking at the country with a completely different view from the one she had first encountered a year ago, being at the mercy of two people she would only ever trust in life to make such a major decision to begin with, had it not been for their persuasion the opportunity itself would not exist. Leading up to this if whenever she seemed uncertain about the prospects of leaving Tia behind, she would ask them whether they still wanted to go ahead with their decision for her to join them. Their response always managed to reassure her how much they cared and they felt she had exhausted her options back in London, being Hita's best friend she naturally only wanted her to be afforded the opportunity of reaching her full potential, Rob reminded her that he loved her immensely and that he needed her to be with him and that he had been patient and had waited long enough for her to be there. Her heart was conflicted but she felt compelled to accomplish what she had already started.

Hita contacted her the following day, having just remembered about the car seats she needed to be brought back to her mum's back in Leicester and she needed it done before she left London. She was felt irritated by Hita's demands, she already had enough to content with and felt Hita was not even considering her time in any of this. Why hadn't she mentioned the car seats before now? Hita not only wanted her to return the car seats, but she had her own ideas about the logistics of it all worked out in her own head and expected her unreasonable requests to be met by her tone, aborting the consideration of anyone else and what they might already have planned that day. Hita stated she wanted both Tia and her to personally ferry the seats over to Leicester and to spend the day with her mum and then stay overnight. The extra demands sounded utterly ridiculous to her, every moment of her time up until her flight had been planned and she had no time to add a night over in Leicester with the six days remaining until her flight. Hita hadn't even had the decency to even ask her if what she may have had on that week, rather than assuming she had nothing to do. At the time of Hita had made contact had she'd of bothered to asked she know she had been waiting inside her local emergency dental hospital and this was her second visit, due to an infection she had developed in her tooth, it had started all of sudden leaving her entire face and neck swollen. Having overdosed on the antibiotics she had been administered only forty-eight hours before, she was now in a race against time to have the offending tooth removed as if things couldn't get any worse.

She had spent over a thousand pounds a year ago trying to repair the problem with root canal surgery and now she was left with the choice of either having it extracted or spending up to another thousand pounds in having another root canal treatment by a specialist. She chose the permanent option she was pleased with her decision, the operation was successful and instantly improved the appearance of her teeth, leaving the inside of her teeth completely symmetrical which she liked. The downside was the operation had revealed she was suffering with dangerous high levels of blood pressure, they were concerned enough to provide her with a letter for her doctor's attention to be fitted with a blood pressure monitor for the next twenty-four hours. The readings highlighted that her blood pressure was only high when awake which was related to stress, however it was important for the blood pressure to drop to regain a normal rate. She would be required to attend the Doctor's the following day to complete another BP reading. If her blood increased any further she may not be able to travel and would be prescribed permanent medication in order to treat the disorder.

She informed Hita that she couldn't guarantee the car seats would make it to Leicester before she arrived in Australia as she was already concerned about the amount of time she had left to organise her own departure, as an alternative she suggested she leave the responsibility with Tia to organise as originally planned. Hita was not compliant and insisted the car seats were returned before she left. Although she was unhappy about Hita's insistence, she quickly put things in to perspective although cumbersome in comparison for the new life she was offering her in Australia. There was no way she would be able to fit in the time to visit Hita's mum before leaving, to save time she arranged a collection and delivery with Parcelforce, it proved to be a sensible option and turned out to be a lot more economical than if she had delivered them herself in person. Hita called a couple of days later to confirm receipt of the car all was well between them, they reconfirmed her flight details, she sounded so excited with the prospect of her arrival, it made her feel excited too and reassured she had made the right decision. Her flight was scheduled to arrive just before midnight, Rob booked a hotel room for them to stay in for the first night and then they would both travel to Hita's a day later. Rob had also taken a couple of days off so he could help her settle in at Hita's.

An hour after speaking to Hita Rob called; he sounded a little down she hadn't realised at first as she was so excited to tell him about her earlier call with Hita. Rob stated that he had just spoken to Paul Hita's husband and he sensed that Paul might have an issue with her staying with them. She asked Rob if he was sure and asked him to recite the conversation that he had had with Paul. Rob stated that he thought the arrangement was that she would stay three days during the week with them and then four days with Rob. Rob stated he felt Paul was now trying to shift all the responsibility of her stay on to him, when he was in the process of trying to sell his house so they could move in to another area and build on a life together. It did not suit her to stay at Rob's house, it was the former family home and she was adamant about never visiting it and Rob was all too aware of how she felt, they had discussed it many times. She didn't even relish the thought of moving in with Rob straight away. Her invite to move to Australia had strictly come from Hita; she hadn't even known Rob when Hita had invited her, although Hita had invited her to stay for a year. She had plans to move in to her own place after a couple of months and would visit Rob at the weekends whenever he was off work. Rob felt this was in contrast to the impression he had, following his talk with Paul and called him back to reconfirm the arrangements. Rob called back later and stated that all was well; he implied Paul had seemed intoxicated but did state he had gotten it wrong earlier and confirmed she was more than welcome to stay with them as arranged as long as she wanted and that Hita would be in touch to reconfirm. He apologised to her that he had not been able to organise a place for them before now and that he had tried his hardest to get a sale, however the realisation of competing with eight hundred other properties were making the prospects of selling his property even more impermeable. The evening before her flight she popped in with Tia to see her Dad she had deliberately put it off until she was no longer able to, she was looking forward to seeing her Dad, but they were unable could it hold it together during the final goodbye.

The day they had all been waiting for was finally here, she had been up since two that morning, but had found it impossible to sleep. An hour later she could lie in bed no longer and began to get ready for her flight. This would be the hardest day of all for her; she hadn't contemplated how difficult the day was going to be, until it was too late. She would be leaving her daughter for a long time and for the very first time and she was concerned. Would she be able to actually go through with getting on the plane? So many were relying on her to do so, including Tia. She was at a point in her life where she needed to do this and explore the possibilities of a future in Australia and consider her own happiness first for once. She had a wonderful man who she truly loved waiting for her, he had been so patient. She felt pulled in so many directions; it was just her luck that the man she was in love with was based in the furthest part of the world.

She questioned why couldn't she have found someone to fall in love with who lived closer. For one moment she wished she could split herself in two. She began to cry every time she thought of Tia her eyes watered. She would miss her daughter terribly, she hadn't even left yet and she was already a mess. They had practically spent the entire week bawling their eyes out and holding on to each other for dear life. The time when they would not have the free liberty to do so was drawing upon them closer and there was nothing they could do to slow that time down, no matter how much they wanted to. They were not ready to be separated but felt they had no option but to. Tia had always been under her mother's shadow; she had just started her first business and was excited about her plans for the future.

She was still recovering from her farewell to her Dad the night before and if anything else was to go by; leaving her daughter would be just as painful. She had never reduced her Dad to tears before, so much so at times he couldn't even speak. She felt totally responsible for the upset she was causing him. Her heart was broken and she was inconsolable after the visit. She would arrange for him to visit once she was settled.

As they drove to the airport she could barely say two words to her daughter before needing the assistance of a tissue, her eyes were bloodshot red from all the crying she was doing. Rob phoned to ensure she was en route to the airport, he spoke to Tia and vowed to keep her mum safe and take care of her as best as he could. She was happy Rob had taken the initiative to do so, it helped to reassure her she was making the right decision to join him. Tia was only able to maintain her composure due to being the designated driver, until then she had struggled to get ready in the morning, every time she stopped to think of her mum leaving her she got terribly upset and couldn't control her tears. She couldn't believe her mum was really leaving her and told her she was the best mum she could ever have hoped to have and that she deserved the chance to find happiness, because she had dedicated her life to her as a mother and now it was her time for her to live own life. She felt this time would be an ideal time for her to find her own independence away from her and was looking forward to the challenges.

As they pulled into the car park at Gatwick Airport the mood became more sombre, she did not want her grief of leaving Tia to be a sad occasion, she felt as if she was going through a bereavement, when in truth it should have been a joyous occasion they had plans to see each other within the next six months. None of that mattered to her now, what mattered was that she would not be able to hold or see her daughter again until then, she began to breakdown again, Tia was visibly upset but able to hold it together. She was proud of how Tia was able to keep it together she displayed a level of strength as a young lady she had not witnessed before and it helped to reinforce her decision was the right one to leave and join Hita and Rob. They stopped off for breakfast and a final drink together to celebrate the beginning of their new lives.

As they approached the departure terminal and walked up to the security gates she found it unbearable to say goodbye, as she walked through the barrier she was a complete mess and could hardly contain herself she felt weak, she turned around to give Tia a final wave, was being consoled by her friend Ruth, she held her hand up and as she waved she told her she would see her soon.

That was the straw that broke the camel's back for her as she hurried off and made her way towards the South Terminal. She popped in to the Ladies en route, reapplied her makeup and freshened up. She was soon seated in the departure lounge where she made her final call to Rob; he was worried she might change her mind at the last minute. Too upset to speak to him on the phone she messaged him to say she was waiting in the lounge area and would soon be boarding the plane. He called her straight away making sure she was okay, she cried silently whilst on the phone to him. Rob understood her grief and did his best to reassure her that he would she was making the right decision and that he would do his utmost to make her happy. He was longing to see her but before doing so; he had a long awaited appointment down the pub and a drink with his name on it to celebrate her new life with him.

***

If you have made it to the end of this novel having read it all, I would like to thank you for taking the time to do so. By now you will be aware that the main character depicted in this novel has only ever been referred to in Third-person character and probably have lots of theories as to the purpose of doing so. The main reason for this approach was due to the personal accounts documented throughout the book actually happened to me, your author Miss S. Lewis-Campbell and welcome to concluding an integral part of my personal testimony. As you digest this exert, I am already in the process of writing the follow-up to this story, which will document my time spent in Australia with an even more spectacular twist that no one, even me saw coming, so be prepared to be even further shocked and enthralled. I look forward to sharing that part of journey with you.

*S. Lewis-Campbell

Acknowledgement - Hita

Many times we have discussed my writings, but I didn't want to bog you down with the details. I thought you may prefer the luxury of being able to read it for yourself when you have the time to. Firstly, I just want to thank you for putting up with me as a best friend over the past twenty-one years and what fun we've had over those years and yet we have both come a long way through our own independent journeys, you especially. It has been a wonderful experience for me seeing you grow in to the success you have become, considering you started off as 'Olive, Raggy Doll,' well look at you now, it makes me extremely proud. Seeing you with your own family now, you are a walking testimony of how to achieve things in the right way. You are a fantastic mother and to think Tia gave you some your first experiences, I also want to thank you for helping me raise her, you will never know how instrumental you were to her upbringing and also to my life when we both needed someone, there you were as surrogate Mother and greatest ally you rolled up those sleeves and got stuck right in, those are the things I can never repay you for, I wonder at times where would we have been without your influence on our lives. I hope someday I will have a similar positive and worthwhile effect on the boys.

Coming to Australia was meant to allow her to get her head together and make some future plans and although they had discussed her visit to Australia over the past ten years. I really thought that ship had sailed for me a long time ago. During my time there this year, it hadn't even entered my mind, I was as shocked at you mentioning it again during my recent visit as I was the other times you have invited me back then. Seeing you for a catch up in Leicester this year, when you stated both Paul and yourself knew I would meet someone there, although you had mentioned it in the past, even though I didn't agree with you both. I never thought that would happen to me on this occasion, never mind at any other time. But as usual you were right and I was so wrong. Although the relationship came with its challenges, yet again you have been so supportive even when you haven't totally been in agreement.

So for that I just want thank you and acknowledge you for being the greatest friend I have ever had and I don't say that lightly, at times unfortunately I couldn't be the friend I felt I should have been to you and for those moments I know I have let you down, or if you may have felt that way I am truly sorry. I don't have any other regrets in life, except for the times I couldn't have been an equally great friend to you as you have and continue to be to me. Thank you for being so instrumental in changing my life for the better, I often ask myself what on earth have I done that been so great for you that you care for me in the way you do, because I do not know. I only wish I could see in me whatever it is you see. One thing I do know is that somewhere deeply embedded within me there is something special worth exploring; otherwise you would have nothing to do with me. I would also like to thank your wonderful family, who from day one have accepted me into their family and have treated me nothing less than one of their own all these years. I am so blessed to have you all in my life, I'm so grateful for everything you have done to get me over to Australia, I will never be able to repay you for it physically, however I am damn sure someday I will make you very proud of me . I don't say this enough but you have it written down here to always reflect on. I love you Hita very much indeed, thank you for making my life what it is today.

NB: Mrs. Mistry, Chan, Crupa, Dina, Paul, Nile, and Ashton, thank you for putting up with our friendship, I know it hasn't been easy for you either, without your love and support; none of this would be possible. I love you all very much indeed.

Acknowledgement – Rob

Well Mr. Robert Van Der Staay, where do I begin? Since the day we met you have become the joy in my life. Similarly to Hita I am unable to see the qualities that you see in me and neither do I care anymore. I am just happy that you chose me and persisted with the course of our relationship. You poor thing! As well as changing my life for the best it's ever been, there have been plenty of times your life has not been so good, because of your involvement with me, but you have always managed to find the resolve to never letting those issues come between us. As a result, you have changed every aspect of your life to accommodate me, when it would have been far simpler for you not to. I hope that in time and in some small way I may be able to make it up to you.

From the moment we met it has been nothing short of a whirlwind between us, we can relate to each other on so many levels. We share so many similar experiences and have many things in common, including our strong connection and because of all we have been through together, we are a strong force to be reckoned with. Becoming a couple has provided you with such an amazing story to tell, I look forward and will be extremely proud to hear you tell it to our future Grandchildren and Great Grandchildren. I'm especially looking forward to hearing you explain to them, how you created your blended family and the travels we shared along the way, just to be together. We still have lots of things to sort out between us, but like we've always said, those issues are just details and that the main thing is that we are together. I hope one day for those that have been affected by us, maybe one day we all be able to sit in the same room together, celebrating you in the way we ought to be. Don't think I haven't noticed the inroads you have been making recently to let this happen sooner rather than later. I know you will decide on what's best when you think the time is right. From my point of view I am not ready yet baby, too much has happened and too much has been said. Putting us in the same environment too soon is not going to be pretty, and it's still fresh and early days. In my opinion we should just wait and see how things unfold and I'd rather it happened naturally, trust me it will be better that way.

Thank you for everything you have done for me and continue to do, I'm really looking forward to us growing old together. I also want to thank you for providing me with the content for this book, had it not been for you I would not have been able to document this wonderful story of ours .

I love you baby and I always will.

Acknowledgement – Dad

To my wonderful Father, because of you I am an accomplished Writer today. Dad from the moment you had me, you have done everything within your power to guide, encourage and protect me.

Your teachings have been invaluable to me. You are very present in my life and although I may not have done everything to make you proud, there is very little I do without wondering how you would feel about it.

There is a lot written in this book which you may not personally agree with, but I know you would be able to relate. I promise you Dad, when you finally get to meet the love of my life within a few weeks, you will understand why I did what I did. I'm hoping that someday you will come and visit and see what I have managed to achieve. I'm looking forward to having that spring in my step again and making it happen. None of the opportunities I have recently been given I would not have been able to achieve without God and to Him I so thankful.

Thanks Dad for always believing in me and standing by me through everything, the Good, the Bad and at times the Ugly. I'm sorry for any disappointments I have personally caused you, because you never deserved to witness any of them. If it wasn't for you I would not have achieve my English degree, I still cannot believe that it took you ten years to talk me into taking it. I'm really sorry for that Dad, it must have been so frustrating for you, but you never ever gave up on me till this very day, in fact you have always believed in me more than I believed in myself and that is still ever so present today. I hope one day I am able to reach my full potential, that's all I ever want out of life and when that day comes, Dad I want you there to witness it. You have been the best parent a daughter could ever wish for thank you for being my strongest supporter Dad and being there for me whenever I've needed you most of all thank you for taking the time to understand me, you're the only parent who just gets me and because of that our bond is so special and always has been.

But mostly Dad I want to thank you for being my biggest supporter and mentor in everything that I do, it has taken your guidance in realizing that my love for the English language and especially for being able to read novels in matter of hours I have learn that gift from you. For as long as I can remember my Dad was always the master in being able to tell a good story whether it concerned a humorous event, a lesson to be learnt or regarding the Good Lord that we serve. I attribute being an Author in my own right as an attainment from you Dad. May God continue to bless you, in continuing to the best Father on Earth. The fact that you are my Dad, I couldn't be anymore more proud, I love you with all my heart Dad.

Shara

Acknowledgement – Tia

Hello my darling daughter one of the hardest things on this earth will be leaving the country to start anew, but I really need to do this. I've needed to live my own life and find out what that is like. It will also give you the time you need to find yourself, without me being over your shoulder every single minute. This way you will be able to grow and really becoming the success you have dreamed of. I'm looking forward to hearing all about it in the future.

The new chapter in our lives will be hard for the both of us, but just remember I've not left you, just the country. I'm only a plane ride away and on the end of the phone, you are welcome wherever I am and I've always maintained that policy, if you're not welcome then I won't be doing it, so please come and visit as often as you can.

I wish you all the best for the future my darling, continue making your old Mum proud. I love you Tia. I only ever had you because my heart was fulfilled the day you were born and that has never changed, go and live your life to the fullest my dear, but never forget your Mother in all that you do and all will work exceed more than you could have ever dreamed of.

Mum. Xxx

35955806R00078

Printed in Poland
by Amazon Fulfillment
Poland Sp. z o.o., Wrocław